The Humourous Lieutenant by John Fletcher

aka Demetrius and Enanthe, Being the Humorous Lieutenant

John Fletcher was born in December, 1579 in Rye, Sussex. He was baptised on December 20th.

As can be imagined details of much of his life and career have not survived and, accordingly, only a very brief indication of his life and works can be given.

Young Fletcher appears at the very young age of eleven to have entered Corpus Christi College at Cambridge University in 1591. There are no records that he ever took a degree but there is some small evidence that he was being prepared for a career in the church.

However what is clear is that this was soon abandoned as he joined the stream of people who would leave University and decamp to the more bohemian life of commercial theatre in London.

The upbringing of the now teenage Fletcher and his seven siblings now passed to his paternal uncle, the poet and minor official Giles Fletcher. Giles, who had the patronage of the Earl of Essex may have been a liability rather than an advantage to the young Fletcher. With Essex involved in the failed rebellion against Elizabeth Giles was also tainted.

By 1606 John Fletcher appears to have equipped himself with the talents to become a playwright. Initially this appears to have been for the Children of the Queen's Revels, then performing at the Blackfriars Theatre.

Fletcher's early career was marked by one significant failure; The Faithful Shepherdess, his adaptation of Giovanni Battista Guarini's Il Pastor Fido, which was performed by the Blackfriars Children in 1608.

By 1609, however, he had found his stride. With his collaborator John Beaumont, he wrote Philaster, which became a hit for the King's Men and began a profitable association between Fletcher and that company. Philaster appears also to have begun a trend for tragicomedy.

By the middle of the 1610s, Fletcher's plays had achieved a popularity that rivalled Shakespeare's and cemented the pre-eminence of the King's Men in Jacobean London. After his frequent early collaborator John Beaumont's early death in 1616, Fletcher continued working, both singly and in collaboration, until his own death in 1625. By that time, he had produced, or had been credited with, close to fifty plays.

Index of Contents
DRAMATIS PERSONAE
THE SCENE: Greece.
PROLOGUE
ACTUS PRIMUS
SCÆNA PRIMA
SCÆNA SECUNDA
ACTUS SECUNDUS

SCÆNA PRIMA
SCÆNA SECUNDA
SCÆNA TERTIA
SCÆNA QUARTA
SCÆNA QUINTA
ACTUS TERTIUS
SCÆNA PRIMA
SCÆNA SECUNDA
SCÆNA TERTIA
SCÆNA QUARTO
SCÆNA QUINTA
SCÆNA SEXTA
ACTUS QUARTUS
SCÆNA PRIMA
SCÆNA SECUNDA
SCÆNA TERTIA
SCÆNA QUARTA
SCÆNA QUINTA
SCÆNA SEXTA
SCAENA SEPTIMA
SCÆNA OCTAVIA
ACTUS QUINTUS
SCÆNA PRIMA
SCÆNA SECUNDA
SCÆNA TERTIA
SCÆNA QUARTA
SCÆNA QUINTA
EPILOGUE
JOHN FLETCHER – A SHORT BIOGRAPHY
JOHN FLETCHER – A CONCISE BIBLIOGRAPHY

DRAMATIS PERSONAE
MEN
King Antigonus, an old Man with young desires.
Demetrius, Son to Antigonus, in love with Celia.
Seleucus   }
Lysimachus   } Three Kings equal sharers with Antigonus of what Alexander had,
Ptolomie   } with united powers opposing Antigonus.
Leontius, a brave old merry Souldier, assistant to Demetrius.
Timon   }
Charinthus   } Servants to Antigonus, and his vices.
Menippus   }
The Humourous Lieutenant.
Gentlemen, Friends and followers of Demetrius.
Three Embassadors, from the three Kings.
Gentlemen-Ushers.

ACTUS PRIMUS

SCÆNA PRIMA

Enter **TWO USHERS** and **GROOMS** with perfumes.

1ST USHER
Round, round, perfume it round, quick, look ye
Diligently the state be right, are these the richest
Cushions? Fie, fie, who waits i'th' wardrobe?

2ND USHER
But pray tell me, do you think for certain
These Embassadours shall have this morning audience?

1ST USHER
They shall have it: Lord that you live at Court
And understand not! I tell you they must have it.

2ND USHER
Upon what necessity?

1ST USHER
Still you are out of the trick of Court, sell your place,

[Enter **LADIES** and **GENTLEMEN**.

And sow your grounds, you are not for this tillage.
Madams, the best way is the upper lodgings,
There you may see at ease.

LADIES
We thank you, Sir.

[Exit **LADIES**, **GENTLEMEN**.

1ST USHER
Would you have all these slighted? who should report then,
The Embassadors were handsome men? his beard
A neat one? the fire of his eyes quicker than lightning,
And when it breaks, as blasting? his legs, though little ones,
Yet movers of a mass of understanding?
Who shall commend their Cloaths? who shall take notice
Of the most wise behaviour of their Feathers?
 e live a raw man here.

2ND USHER
I think I do so.

[Enter **TWO CITIZENS** and **WIVES**.

1ST USHER
Why, whither would ye all press?

1ST CITIZEN
Good Master Usher.

2ND CITIZEN
My wife, and some few of my honest neighbours, here.

1ST USHER
Prethee begone thou and thy honest Neighbours,
Thou lookst like an Ass, why, whither would you fish face?

2ND CITIZEN
If I might have
But the honour to see you at my poor house, Sir,
A Capon bridled and sadled, I'le assure your worship,
A shoulder of Mutton and a pottle of Wine, Sir,
I know your Brother, he was like ye,
And shot the best at Buts—

1ST USHER
A—upon thee.

2ND CITIZEN
Some Musick I'le assure you too,
My toy, Sir, can play o'th' Virginals.

1ST USHER
Prethee good toy,
Take away thy shoulder of Mutton, it is flie-blown,
And shoulder take thy flap along, here's no place for ye;
Nay then you had best be knock'd.

[Exit **CITIZENS**.

[Enter **CELIA**.

CELIA
I wou'd fain see him,
The glory of this place makes me remember,
But dye those thoughts, dye all but my desires,
Even those to death are sick too; he's not here,

Nor how my eyes may guide me—

1ST USHER
What's your business?
Who keeps the outward door there? here's fine shuffling,
You wastcoateer you must go back.

CELIA
There is not,
There cannot be, six days and never see me?
There must not be desire; Sir, do you think
That if you had a Mistris—

1ST USHER
Death, she is mad.

CELIA
And were yourself an honest man? it cannot—

1ST USHER
What a Devil hast thou to do with me or my honesty?
Will you be jogging, good nimble tongue,
My fellow door-keeper.

2ND USHER
Prethee let her alone,

1ST USHER
The King is coming,
And shall we have an agent from the Suburbs
Come to crave audience too?

CELIA
Before I thought ye
To have a little breeding, some tang of Gentry;
But now I take ye plainly,
Without the help of any perspective,
For that ye cannot alter.

1ST USHER
What's that?

CELIA
An Ass, Sir, you bray as like one,
And by my troth, me thinks as ye stand now,
Considering who to kick next, you appear to me
Just with that kind of gravity, and wisdom;
Your place may bear the name of Gentleman,

But if ever any of that butter stick to your bread—

2ND USHER
You must be modester.

CELIA
Let him use me nobler,
And wear good Cloaths to do good Offices;
They hang upon a fellow of his vertue,
As though they hung on Gibbets.

2ND USHER
A perillous wench.

1ST USHER
Thrust her into a corner, I'le no more on her.

2ND USHER
You have enough, go pretty Maid, stand close,
And use that little tongue, with a little more temper.

CELIA
I thank ye, Sir.

2ND USHER
When the show's past,
I'le have ye into the Cellar, there we'll dine.
A very pretty wench, a witty Rogue,
And there we'll be as merry; can ye be merry?

CELIA
O very merry.

2ND USHER
Only our selves; this churlish fellow shall not know.

CELIA
By no means.

2ND USHER
And can you love a little?

CELIA
Love exceedingly:
I have cause to love you, dear Sir.

2ND USHER
Then I'le carry ye,

And shew you all the pictures, and the hangings,
The Lodgings, Gardens, and the walks: and then, sweet,
You shall tell me where you lye.

CELIA
Yes marry will I.

2ND USHER
And't shall go hard but I'le send ye a Venison Pasty,
And bring a bottle of wine along.

1ST USHER
Make room there,

2ND USHER
Room there afore; stand close, the train is coming.

[Enter **KING ANTIGONUS, TIMON, CHARINTHUS, MENIPPUS**.

CELIA
Have I yet left a beauty to catch fools?
Yet, yet, I see him not. O what a misery
Is love, expected long, deluded longer!

ANTIGONUS
Conduct in the Embassadors.

1ST USHER
Make room there.

ANTIGONUS
They shall not wait long answer—

[Flourish.

CELIA
Yet he comes not.

[Enter **THREE EMBASSADORS**.

Why are eyes set on these, and multitudes
Follow to make these wonders? O good gods!
What would these look like if my love were here?
But I am fond, forgetful.

ANTIGONUS
Now your grievance,
Speak short, and have as short dispatch.

1ST EMBASSADOR
Then thus, Sir:
In all our Royal Masters names, We tell you,
Ye have done injustice, broke the bonds of concord,
And from their equal shares, from Alexander
Parted, and so possess'd, not like a Brother,
But as an open Enemy, Ye have hedged in
Whole Provinces, man'd and maintain'd these injuries;
And daily with your sword (though they still honour ye)
Make bloudy inroads, take Towns, and ruin Castles,
And still their sufFerance feels the weight.

2ND EMBASSADOR
Think of that love, great Sir, that honor'd friendship
Your self held with our Masters, think of that strength
When you were all one body, all one mind;
When all your swords struck one way, when your angers,
Like so many brother Billows rose together,
And curling up your foaming Crests, defied
Even mighty Kings, and in their falls entomb'd 'em;
O think of these; and you that have been Conquerours,
That ever led your Fortunes open ey'd,
Chain'd fast by confidence; you that fame courted,
Now ye want Enemies and men to match ye,
Let not your own Swords seek your ends to shame ye.

[Enter **DEMETRIUS** with a Javelin, and **GENTLEMEN**.

3RD EMBASSADOR
Choose which you will, or Peace or War,
We come prepar'd for either.

1st USHER
Room for the Prince there.

CELIA
Was it the Prince they said? how my heart trembled!
'Tis he indeed; what a sweet noble fierceness
Dwells in his eyes! young Meleager like,
When he return'd from slaughter of the Boar,
Crown'd with the loves and honours of the people,
With all the gallant youth of Greece, he looks now,
Who could deny him love?

DEMETRIUS
Hail Royal Father.

ANTIGONUS
Ye are welcome from your sport, Sir, do you see this Gent.
You that bring Thunders in your mouths, and Earthquakes
To shake and totter my designs? can you imagine
(You men of poor and common apprehensions)
While I admit this man, my Son, this nature
That in one look carries more fire, and fierceness,
Than all your Masters in their lives; dare I admit him,
Admit him thus, even to my side, my bosom,
When he is fit to rule, when all men cry him,
And all hopes hang about his head; thus place him,
His weapon hatched in bloud, all these attending
When he shall make their fortunes, all as sudden
In any expedition he shall point 'em,
As arrows from a Tartars bow, and speeding,
Dare I do this, and fear an enemy?
Fear your great Master? yours? or yours?

DEMETRIUS
O Hercules!
Who saies you do, Sir? Is there any thing
In these mens faces, or their Masters actions,
Able to work such wonders?

CELIA
Now he speaks:
O I could dwell upon that tongue for ever.

DEMETRIUS
You call 'em Kings, they never wore those Royalties,
Nor in the progress of their lives arriv'd yet
At any thought of King: Imperial dignities,
And powerful God-like actions, fit for Princes
They can no more put on, and make 'em sit right,
Than I can with this mortal hand hold Heaven:
Poor petty men, nor have I yet forgot
The chiefest honours time, and merit gave 'em:
Lisimachus your Master, at the best,
His highest, and his hopeful'st Dignities
Was but grand-master of the Elephants;
Seleuchus of the Treasure; and for Ptolomey,
A thing not thought on then, scarce heard of yet,
Some Master of Ammunition: and must these men—

CELIA
What a brave confidence flows from his spirit!
O sweet young man!

DEMETRIUS
Must these, hold pace with us,
And on the same file hang their memories?
Must these examine what the wills of Kings are?
Prescribe to their designs, and chain their actions
To their restraints? be friends, and foes when they please?
Send out their Thunders, and their menaces,
As if the fate of mortal things were theirs?
Go home good men, and tell your Masters from us,
We do 'em too much honour to force from 'em
Their barren Countries, ruin their vast Cities,
And tell 'em out of love, we mean to leave 'em
(Since they will needs be Kings) no more to tread on,
Than they have able wits, and powers to manage,
And so we shall befriend 'em. Ha! what does she there?

EMBASSADOR
This is your answer King?

ANTIGONUS
'Tis like to prove so.

DEMETRIUS
Fie, sweet, what makes you here?

CELIA
Pray ye do not chide me.

DEMETRIUS
You do your self much wrong and me.
I feel my fault which only was committed
Through my dear love to you: I have not seen ye,
And how can I live then? I have not spoke to ye—

DEMETRIUS
I know this week ye have not; I will redeem all.
You are so tender now; think where you are, sweet.

CELIA
What other light have I left?

DEMETRIUS
Prethee Celia,
Indeed I'le see you presently.

CELIA
I have done, Sir:
You will not miss?

DEMETRIUS
By this, and this, I will not.

CELIA
'Tis in your will and I must be obedient.

DEMETRIUS
No more of these assemblies.

CELIA
I am commanded.

1ST USHER
Room for the Lady there: Madam, my service—

1ST GENTLEMAN
My Coach an't please you Lady.

2ND USHER
Room before there.

2ND GENTLEMAN
The honour, Madam, but to wait upon you—
My servants and my state.

CELIA
Lord, how they flock now!
Before I was afraid they would have beat me;
How these flies play i'th' Sun-shine! pray ye no services,
Or if ye needs must play the Hobby-horses,
Seek out some beauty that affects 'em: farewel,
Nay pray ye spare: Gentlemen I am old enough
To go alone at these years, without crutches.

[Exit.

2ND USHER
Well I could curse now: but that will not help me,
I made as sure account of this wench now, immediately,
Do but consider how the Devil has crost me,
Meat for my Master she cries, well—

3RD EMBASSADOR
Once more, Sir,
We ask your resolutions: Peace or War yet?

DEMETRIUS

War, War, my noble Father.

1ᔆᵀ EMBASSADOR
Thus I fling it:
And fair ey'd peace, farewel.

ANTIGONUS
You have your answer;
Conduct out the Embassadours, and give 'em Convoyes.

DEMETRIUS
Tell your high hearted Masters, they shall not seek us,
Nor cool i'th' field in expectation of us,
We'l ease your men those marches: In their strengths,
And full abilities of mind and courage,
We'l find 'em out, and at their best trim buckle with 'em.

3ᴿᴰ EMBASSADOR
You will find so hot a Souldier's welcome, Sir,
Your favour shall not freeze.

2ᴺᴰ EMBASSADOR
A forward Gentleman,
Pity the Wars should bruise such hopes—

ANTIGONUS
Conduct em—

[Exit **EMBASSADOR**.

Now, for this preparation: where's Leontius?
Call him in presently: for I mean in person Gentlemen
My self, with my old fortune—

DEMETRIUS
Royal Sir:
Thus low I beg this honour: fame already
Hath every where rais'd Trophies to your glory,
And conquest now grown old, and weak with following
The weary marches and the bloody shocks
You daily set her in: 'tis now scarce honour
For you that never knew to fight, but conquer,
To sparkle such poor people: the Royal Eagle
When she hath tri'd her young ones 'gainst the Sun,
And found 'em right; next teacheth 'em to prey,
How to command on wing, and check below her
Even Birds of noble plume; I am your own, Sir,
You have found my spirit, try it now, and teach it

To stoop whole Kingdoms: leave a little for me:
Let not your glory be so greedy, Sir,
To eat up all my hopes; you gave me life,
If to that life you add not what's more lasting
A noble name, for man, you have made a shadow:
Bless me this day: bid me go on, and lead,
Bid me go on, no less fear'd, than Antigonus,
And to my maiden sword, tye fast your fortune:
I know 'twill fight it self then: dear Sir, honour me:
Never fair Virgin long'd so.

ANTIGONUS
Rise, and command then,
And be as fortunate, as I expect ye:
I love that noble will; your young companions
Bred up and foster'd with ye, I hope Demetrius,
You will make souldiers too: they must not leave ye.

[Enter **LEONTIUS**.

2ND GENTLEMAN
Never till life leave us, Sir.

ANTIGONUS
O Leontius,
Here's work for you in hand.

LEONTIUS
I am ev'n right glad, Sir.
For by my troth, I am now grown old with idleness;
I hear we shall abroad, Sir.

ANTIGONUS
Yes, and presently,
But who think you commands now?

LEONTIUS
Who commands, Sir?
Methinks mine eye should guide me: can there be
(If you your self will spare him so much honour)
Any found out to lead before your Armies,
So full of faith, and fire, as brave Demetrius?
King Philips Son, at his years was an old Souldier,
'Tis time his Fortune be o' wing, high time, Sir,
So many idle hours, as here he loyters,
So many ever-living names he loses,
I hope 'tis he.

ANTIGONUS
'Tis he indeed, and nobly
He shall set forward: draw you all those Garrisons
Upon the frontiers as you pass: to those
Joyn these in pay at home, our ancient souldiers,
And as you go press all the Provinces.

LEONTIUS
We shall not need;
Believe, this hopefull Gentleman
Can want no swords, nor honest hearts to follow him,
We shall be full, no fear Sir.

ANTIGONUS
You Leontius,
Because you are an old and faithfull servant,
And know the wars, with all his vantages,
Be near to his instructions, lest his youth
Lose valours best companion, staid discretion,
Shew where to lead, to lodge, to charge with safetie;
In execution not to break, nor scatter,
But with a provident anger, follow nobly:
Not covetous of blood, and death, but honour,
Be ever near his watches; cheer his labours,
And where his hope stands fair, provoke his valour;
Love him, and think it no dishonour (my Demetrius)
To wear this Jewel near thee; he is a tri'd one,
And one that even in spight of time, that sunk him,
And frosted up his strength, will yet stand by thee,
And with the proudest of thine Enemies
Exchange for bloud, and bravely: take his Counsel.

LEONTIUS
Your grace hath made me young again, and wanton.

ANTIGONUS [to **MINIPPUS**]
She must be known and suddenly:
Do ye know her?

GENTLEMAN, CHARINTHUS
No, believe Sir.

ANTIGONUS
Did you observe her, Timon?

TIMON
I look'd on her,
But what she is—

ANTIGONUS
I must have that found.
Come in and take your leave.

TIMON
And some few Prayers along.

DEMETRIUS
I know my duty,

[Exit **ANTIGONUS**.

You shall be half my Father.

LEONTIUS
All your Servant:
Come Gentlemen, you are resolv'd I am sure
To see these wars.

1ST GENTLEMAN
We dare not leave his fortunes,
Though most assur'd death hung round about us.

LEONTIUS
That bargain's yet to make;
Be not too hasty, when ye face the Enemie,
Nor too ambitious to get honour instantly,
But charge within your bounds, and keep close bodies,
And you shall see what sport we'l make these mad-caps;
You shall have game enough, I warrant ye,
Every mans Cock shall fight.

DEMETRIUS
I must go see Sir:
Brave Sir, as soon as I have taken leave,
I'le meet you in the park;
Draw the men thither,
Wait you upon Leontius.

GENTLEMAN
We'l attend Sir.

LEONTIUS
But I beseech your Grace, with speed; the sooner
We are i'th' field.—

DEMETRIUS

You could not please me better.

[Exit.

LEONTIUS
You never saw the wars yet?

GENTLEMAN
Not yet Colonel.

LEONTIUS
These foolish Mistresses do so hang about ye,
So whimper, and so hug, I know it Gentlemen,
And so intice ye, now ye are i'th' bud;
And that sweet tilting war, with eyes and kisses,
Th' alarms of soft vows, and sighs, and fiddle faddles,
Spoils all our trade: you must forget these knick knacks,
A woman at some time of year, I grant ye
She is necessarie; but make no business of her.
How now Lieutenant?

[Enter **LIEUTENANT**.

LIEUTENANT
Oh Sir, as ill as ever;
We shall have wars they say; they are mustring yonder:
Would we were at it once: fie, how it plagues me.

LEONTIUS
Here's one has served now under Captain Cupid,
And crackt a Pike in's youth: you see what's come on't.

LIEUTENANT
No, my disease will never prove so honourable.

LEONTIUS
Why sure, thou hast the best pox.

LIEUTENANT
If I have 'em,
I am sure I got 'em in the best company;
They are pox of thirty Coats.

LEONTIUS
Thou hast mewed 'em finely:
Here's a strange fellow now, and a brave fellow,
If we may say so of a pocky fellow,
(Which I believe we may) this poor Lieutenant;

Whether he have the scratches, or the scabs,
Or what a Devil it be, I'le say this for him,
There fights no braver souldier under Sun, Gentlemen;
Show him an Enemie, his pain's forgot straight;
And where other men by beds and bathes have ease,
And easie rules of Physick; set him in a danger,
A danger, that's a fearfull one indeed,
Ye rock him, and he will so play about ye,
Let it be ten to one he ne'er comes off again,
Ye have his heart: and then he works it bravely,
And throughly bravely: not a pang remembre'd:
I have seen him do such things, belief would shrink at.

GENTLEMAN
'Tis strange he should do all this, and diseas'd so.

LEONTIUS
I am sure 'tis true: Lieutenant, canst thou drink well?

LIEUTENANT
Would I were drunk, dog-drunk, I might not feel this backward?

GENTLEMAN
I would take Physick.

LIEUTENANT
But I would know my disease first.

LEONTIUS
Why? it may be the Colique: canst thou blow

LIEUTENANT
There's never a bag-pipe in the Kingdom better.

GENTLEMAN
Is't not a pleuresie?

LIEUTENANT
'Tis any thing
That has the Devil, and death in't: will ye march Gentlemen?
The Prince has taken leave.

LEONTIUS
How know ye that?

LIEUTENANT
I saw him leave the Court, dispatch his followers,
And met him after in a by street: I think

He has some wench, or such a toy, to lick over
Before he go: would I had such another
To draw this foolish pain down.

LEONTIUS
Let's away Gentlemen,
For sure the Prince will stay on us.

GENTLEMAN
We'l attend Sir.

[Exeunt.

SCÆNA SECUNDA

Enter **DEMETRIUS** and **CELIA**.

CELIA
Must ye needs go?

DEMETRIUS
Or stay with all dishonour.

CELIA
Are there not men enough to fight?

DEMETRIUS
Fie Celia.
This ill becomes the noble love you bear me;
Would you have your love a coward?

CELIA
No; believe Sir,
I would have him fight, but not so far off from me.

DEMETRIUS
Wouldst have it thus? or thus?

CELIA
If that be fighting—

DEMETRIUS
Ye wanton fool: when I come home again
I'le fight with thee, at thine own weapon Celia,
And conquer thee too.

CELIA
That you have done already,
You need no other Arms to me, but these Sir;
But will you fight your self Sir?

DEMETRIUS
Thus deep in bloud wench,
And through the thickest ranks of Pikes.

CELIA
Spur bravely
Your firie Courser, beat the troops before ye,
And cramb the mouth of death with executions.

DEMETRIUS
I would do more than these: But prethee tell me,
Tell me my fair, where got'st thou this male Spirit?
I wonder at thy mind.

CELIA
Were I a man then,
You would wonder more.

DEMETRIUS
Sure thou wouldst prove a Souldier,
And some great Leader.

CELIA
Sure I should do somewhat;
And the first thing I did, I should grow envious,
Extreamly envious of your youth, and honour.

DEMETRIUS
And fight against me?

CELIA
Ten to one, I should do it.

DEMETRIUS
Thou wouldst not hurt me?

CELIA
In this mind I am in
I think I should be hardly brought to strike ye,
Unless 'twere thus; but in my mans mind—

DEMETRIUS
What?

CELIA
I should be friends with you too,
Now I think better.

DEMETRIUS
Ye are a tall Souldier:
Here, take these, and these;
This gold to furnish ye, and keep this bracelet;
Why do you weep now?
You a masculine Spirit?

CELIA
No, I confess, I am a fool, a woman:
And ever when I part with you—

DEMETRIUS
You shall not,
These tears are like prodigious signs, my sweet one,
I shall come back, loaden with fame, to honour thee.

CELIA
I hope you shall:
But then my dear Demetrius,
When you stand Conquerour, and at your mercy
All people bow, and all things wait your sentence;
Say then your eye (surveying all your conquest)
Finds out a beautie, even in sorrow excellent,
A constant face, that in the midst of ruine
With a forc'd smile, both scorns at fate, and fortune:
Say you find such a one, so nobly fortified,
And in her figure all the sweets of nature?

DEMETRIUS
Prethee,
No more of this, I cannot find her.

CELIA
That shews as far beyond my wither'd beauty;
And will run mad to love ye too.

DEMETRIUS
Do you fear me,
And do you think, besides this face, this beauty,
This heart, where all my hopes are lock'd—

CELIA
I dare not:

No sure, I think ye honest; wondrous honest.
Pray do not frown, I'le swear ye are.

DEMETRIUS
Ye may choose.

CELIA
But how long will ye be away?

DEMETRIUS
I know not.

CELIA
I know you are angry now: pray look upon me:
I'le ask no more such questions.

DEMETRIUS
The Drums beat,
I can no longer stay.

CELIA
They do but call yet:
How fain you would leave my Company?

DEMETRIUS
I wou'd not,
Unless a greater power than love commanded,
Commands my life, mine honour.

CELIA
But a little.

DEMETRIUS
Prethee farewel, and be not doubtfull of me.

CELIA
I would not have ye hurt: and ye are so ventrous—
But good sweet Prince preserve your self, fight nobly,
But do not thrust this body, 'tis not yours now,
'Tis mine, 'tis only mine: do not seek wounds, Sir,
For every drop of blood you bleed—

DEMETRIUS
I will Celia,
I will be carefull.

CELIA
My heart, that loves ye dearly.

DEMETRIUS
Prethee no more, we must part:

[Drums a March.

Hark, they march now.

CELIA
Pox on these bawling Drums: I am sure you'l kiss me,
But one kiss? what a parting's this?

DEMETRIUS
Here take me,
And do what thou wilt with me, smother me;
But still remember, if your fooling with me,
Make me forget the trust—

CELIA
I have done: farewel Sir,
Never look back, you shall not stay, not a minute.

DEMETRIUS
I must have one farewel more.

CELIA
No, the Drums beat;
I dare not slack your honour; not a hand more,
Only this look; the gods preserve, and save ye.

ACTUS SECUNDUS

SCÆNA PRIMA

Enter **ANTIGONUS, CHARINTHUS, TIMON.**

ANTIGONUS
What, have ye found her out?

CHARINTHUS
We have hearkned after her.

ANTIGONUS
What's that to my desire?

CHARINTHUS

Your grace must give us time,
And a little means.

TIMON
She is sure a stranger,
If she were bred or known here—

ANTIGONUS
Your dull endeavours

[Enter **MENIPPUS**.

Should never be employ'd. Welcom Menippus.

MENIPPUS
I have found her Sir,
I mean the place she is lodg'd in; her name is Celia,
And much adoe I had to purchase that too.

ANTIGONUS
Dost think Demetrius loves her?

MENIPPUS
Much I fear it,
But nothing that way yet can win for certain.
I'le tell your grace within this hour.

ANTIGONUS
A stranger?

MENIPPUS
Without all doubt.

ANTIGONUS
But how should he come to her?

MENIPPUS
There lies the marrow of the matter hid yet.

ANTIGONUS
Hast thou been with thy wife?

MENIPPUS
No Sir, I am going to her.

ANTIGONUS
Go and dispatch, and meet me in the garden,
And get all out ye can.

[Exit.

MENIPPUS
I'le doe my best Sir.

[Exit.

TIMON
Blest be thy wife, thou wert an arrant ass else.

CHARINTHUS
I, she is a stirring woman indeed:
There's a brain Brother.

TIMON
There's not a handsom wench of any mettle
Within an hundred miles, but her intelligence
Reaches her, and out-reaches her, and brings her
As confidently to Court, as to a sanctuary:
What had his mouldy brains ever arriv'd at,
Had not she beaten it out o'th' Flint to fasten him?
They say she keeps an office of Concealments:
There is no young wench, let her be a Saint,
Unless she live i'th' Center, but she finds her,
And every way prepares addresses to her:
If my wife would have followed her course Charinthus,
Her lucky course, I had the day before him:
O what might I have been by this time, Brother?
But she (forsooth) when I put these things to her,
These things of honest thrift, groans, O my conscience,
The load upon my conscience, when to make us cuckolds,
They have no more burthen than a brood-goose, Brother;
But let's doe what we can, though this wench fail us,
Another of a new way will be lookt at:
Come, let's abroad, and beat our brains, time may
For all his wisdom, yet give us a day.

[Exeunt.

SCÆNA SECUNDA

Drum within, Alarm, Enter **DEMETRIUS** and **LEONTIUS**.

DEMETRIUS
I will not see 'em fall thus, give me way Sir,

I shall forget you love me else.

LEONTIUS
Will ye lose all?
For me to be forgotten, to be hated,
Nay never to have been a man, is nothing,
So you, and those we have preserv'd from slaughter
Come safely off.

DEMETRIUS
I have lost my self.

LEONTIUS
You are cozen'd.

DEMETRIUS
And am most miserable.

LEONTIUS
There's no man so, but he that makes himself so.

DEMETRIUS
I will goe on.

LEONTIUS
You must not: I shall tell you then,
And tell you true, that man's unfit to govern,
That cannot guide himself: you lead an Army?
That have not so much manly suff'rance left ye,
To bear a loss?

DEMETRIUS
Charge but once more Leontius,
My friends and my companions are engag'd all.

LEONTIUS
Nay give 'em lost, I saw 'em off their horses,
And the enemy master of their Arms; nor could then
The policie, nor strength of man redeem 'em.

DEMETRIUS
And shall I know this, and stand fooling?

LEONTIUS
By my dead Fathers soul you stir not, Sir,
Or if you doe, you make your way through me first.

DEMETRIUS

Thou art a Coward.

LEONTIUS
To prevent a Madman.
None but your Fathers Son, durst call me so,
'Death if he did—Must I be scandal'd by ye,
That hedg'd in all the helps I had to save ye?
That, where there was a valiant weapon stirring,
Both search'd it out, and singl'd it, unedg'd it,
For fear it should bite you, am I a coward?
Go, get ye up, and tell 'em ye are the Kings Son;
Hang all your Ladys favours on your Crest,
And let them fight their shares; spur to destruction,
You cannot miss the way: be bravely desperate,
And your young friends before ye, that lost this battel,
Your honourable friends, that knew no order,
Cry out, Antigonus, the old Antigonus,
The wise and fortunate Antigonus,
The great, the valiant, and the fear'd Antigonus,
Has sent a desperate son, without discretion
To bury in an hour his age of honour.

DEMETRIUS
I am ashamed.

LEONTIUS
'Tis ten to one, I die with ye:
The coward will not long be after ye;
I scorn to say I saw you fall, sigh for ye,
And tell a whining tale, some ten years after
To boyes and girles in an old chimney corner,
Of what a Prince we had, how bravely spirited;
How young and fair he fell: we'l all go with ye,
And ye shall see us all, like sacrifices
In our best trim, fill up the mouth of ruine.
Will this faith satisfie your folly? can this show ye
'Tis not to die we fear, but to die poorly,
To fall, forgotten, in a multitude?
If you will needs tempt fortune now she has held ye,
Held ye from sinking up.

DEMETRIUS
Pray do not kill me,
These words pierce deeper than the wounds I suffer,
The smarting wounds of loss.

LEONTIUS
Ye are too tender;

Fortune has hours of loss, and hours of honour,
And the most valiant feel them both: take comfort,
The next is ours, I have a soul descries it:
The angry bull never goes back for breath
But when he means to arm his fury double.
Let this day set, but not the memorie,
And we shall find a time: How now Lieutenant?

[Enter **LIEUTENANT**.

LIEUTENANT
I know not: I am mall'd: we are bravely beaten,
All our young gallants lost.

LEONTIUS
Thou art hurt.

LIEUTENANT
I am pepper'd,
I was i'th' midst of all: and bang'd of all hands:
They made an anvile of my head, it rings yet;
Never so thresh'd: do you call this fame? I have fam'd it;
I have got immortal fame, but I'le no more on't;
I'le no such scratching Saint to serve hereafter;
O' my conscience I was kill'd above twenty times,
And yet I know not what a Devil's in't,
I crawled away, and lived again still; I am hurt plaguily,
But now I have nothing near so much pain Colonel,
They have sliced me for that maladie.

DEMETRIUS
All the young men lost?

LIEUTENANT
I am glad you are here: but they are all i'th' pound sir,
They'l never ride o're other mens corn again, I take it,
Such frisking, and such flaunting with their feathers,
And such careering with their Mistres favours;
And here must he be pricking out for honour,
And there got he a knock, and down goes pilgarlick,
Commends his soul to his she-saint, and Exit.
Another spurs in there, cryes make room villains,
I am a Lord, scarce spoken, but with reverence
A Rascal takes him o're the face, and fells him;
There lyes the Lord, the Lord be with him.

LEONTIUS
Now Sir,

Do you find this truth?

DEMETRIUS
I would not.

LIEUTENANT
Pox upon it,
They have such tender bodies too; such Culisses,
That one good handsom blow breaks 'em a pieces.

LEONTIUS
How stands the Enemy?

LIEUTENANT
Even cool enough too:
For to say truth he has been shrewdly heated,
The Gentleman no doubt will fall to his jewlips.

LEONTIUS
He marches not i'th' tail on's.

LIEUTENANT
No, plague take him,
He'l kiss our tails as soon; he looks upon us,
As if he would say, if ye will turn again, friends,
We will belabor you a little better,
And beat a little more care into your coxcombs.
Now shall we have damnable Ballads out against us,
Most wicked madrigals: and ten to one, Colonel,
Sung to such lowsie, lamentable tunes.

LEONTIUS
Thou art merry,
How e're the game goes: good Sir be not troubled,
A better day will draw this back again.
Pray go, and cheer those left, and lead 'em off,
They are hot, and weary.

DEMETRIUS
I'le doe any thing.

LEONTIUS
Lieutenant, send one presently away
To th' King, and let him know our state: and hark ye,
Be sure the messenger advise his Majestie
To comfort up the Prince: he's full of sadness.

LIEUTENANT

When shall I get a Surgeon? this hot weather,
Unless I be well pepper'd, I shall stink, Colonel.

LEONTIUS
Go, I'le prepare thee one.

LIEUTENANT
If ye catch me then,
Fighting again, I'le eat hay with a horse.

[Exit.

SCÆNA TERTIA

Enter **LEUCIPPE** reading and **TWO MAIDS** at a Table writing.

LEUCIPPE
Have ye written to Merione?

1ST MAID
Yes, Madam.

LEUCIPPE
And let her understand the hopes she has,
If she come speedilie—

1ST MAID
All these are specified.

LEUCIPPE
And of the chain is sent her,
And the rich stuff to make her shew more handsom here?

1ST MAID
All this is done, Madam.

LEUCIPPE
What have you dispatcht there?

2ND MAID
A letter to the Country maid, and't please ye.

LEUCIPPE
A pretty girle, but peevish, plaguy peevish:
Have ye bought the embroydered gloves, and that purse for her,
And the new Curle?

2ND MAID
They are ready packt up Madam.

LEUCIPPE
Her maiden-head will yield me; let me see now;
She is not fifteen they say: for her complexion—
Cloe, Cloe, Cloe, here, I have her,
Cloe, the Daughter of a Country Gentleman;
Her age upon fifteen: now her complexion,
A lovely brown; here 'tis; eyes black and rolling,
The body neatly built: she strikes a Lute well,
Sings most inticingly, these helps consider'd,
Her maiden-head will amount to some three hundred,
Or three hundred and fifty Crowns, 'twill bear it handsomly.
Her Father's poor, some little share deducted,
To buy him a hunting Nag; I, 'twill be pretty.
Who takes care of the Merchants Wife?

1ST MAID
I have wrought her.

LEUCIPPE
You know for whom she is?

1ST MAID
Very well, Madam,
Though very much ado I had to make her
Apprehend that happiness.

LEUCIPPE
These Kind are subtile;
Did she not cry and blubber when you urg'd her?

1ST MAID
O most extreamly, and swore she would rather perish.

LEUCIPPE
Good signs, very good signs,
Symptoms of easie nature.
Had she the Plate?

1ST MAID
She lookt upon't, and left it,
And turn'd again, and view'd it.

LEUCIPPE
Very well still.

1ST MAID
At length she was content to let it lye there,
Till I call'd for't, or so.

LEUCIPPE
She will come?

1ST MAID
Do you take me
For such a Fool, I would part without that promise?

LEUCIPPE
The Chamber's next the Park.

1ST MAID
The Widow, Madam,
You bad me look upon.

LEUCIPPE
Hang her, she is musty:
She is no mans meat; besides, she's poor and sluttish:
Where lyes old Thisbe now, you are so long now—

2ND MAID
Thisbe, Thisbe, Thisbe, agent Thisbe, O I have her,
She lyes now in Nicopolis.

LEUCIPPE
Dispatch a Packet,
And tell her, her Superiour here commands her
The next month not to fail, but see deliver'd
Here to our use, some twenty young and handsom,
As also able Maids, for the Court service,
As she will answer it: we are out of beauty,
Utterly out, and rub the time away here
With such blown stuff, I am asham'd to send it.

[Knock within

Who's that? look out, to your business, Maid,
There's nothing got by idleness: there is a Lady,
Which if I can but buckle with, Altea,
A, A, A, A, Altea young, and married,
And a great lover of her husband, well,
Not to be brought to Court! say ye so? I am sorry,
The Court shall be brought to you then; how now, who is't?

1ST MAID
An ancient woman, with a maid attending,
A pretty Girl, but out of Cloaths; for a little money,
It seems she would put her to your bringing up, Madam.

[Enter **WOMAN** and **PHEBE**.

LEUCIPPE
Let her come in. Would you ought with us, good woman?
I pray be short, we are full of business.

WOMAN
I have a tender Girl here, an't please your honour.

LEUCIPPE
Very well.

WOMAN
That hath a great desire to serve your worship.

LEUCIPPE
It may be so; I am full of Maids.

WOMAN
She is young forsooth—
And for her truth; and as they say her bearing.

LEUCIPPE
Ye say well; come ye hither maid, let me feel your pulse,
'Tis somewhat weak, but Nature will grow stronger,
Let me see your leg, she treads but low i'th' Pasterns.

WOMAN
A cork Heel, Madam.

LEUCIPPE
We know what will do it,
Without your aim, good woman; what do you pitch her at?
She's but a slight toy—cannot hold out long.

WOMAN
Even what you think is meet.

LEUCIPPE
Give her ten Crowns, we are full of business,
She is a poor Woman, let her take a Cheese home.
Enter the wench i' th' Office.

[Exit **WOMAN** and **1ST MAID**.

2ND MAID
What's your name, Sister?

PHEBE
Phebe, forsooth.

LEUCIPPE
A pretty name; 'twill do well:
Go in, and let the other Maid instruct you, Phebe.

[Exit **PHEBE**.

Let my old Velvet skirt be made fit for her.
I'll put her into action for a Wast-coat;
And when I have rigg'd her up once, this small Pinnace
Shall sail for Gold, and good store too; who's there?

[Knock within

Lord, shall we never have any ease in this world!
Still troubled! still molested! what would you have?

[Enter **MENIPPUS**.

I cannot furnish you faster than I am able,
And ye were my Husband a thousand times, I cannot do it.
At least a dozen posts are gone this morning
For several parts of the Kingdom: I can do no more
But pay 'em, and instruct 'em.

MENIPPUS
Prithee, good sweet heart,
I come not to disturb thee, nor discourage thee,
I know thou labour'st truly: hark in thine ear.

LEUCIPPE
Ha!
What do you make so dainty on't? look there
I am an Ass, I can do nothing.

MENIPPUS
Celia?
I, this is she; a stranger born.

LEUCIPPE
What would you give for more now?

MENIPPUS
Prithee, my best Leucippe, there's much hangs on't,
Lodg'd at the end of Mars's street? that's true too;
At the sack of such a Town, by such a Souldier
Preserv'd a Prisoner: and by Prince Demetrius
Bought from that man again, maintain'd and favour'd:
How came you by this knowledg?

LEUCIPPE
Poor, weak man,
I have a thousand eyes, when thou art sleeping,
Abroad, and full of business.

MENIPPUS
You never try'd her?

LEUCIPPE
No, she is beyond my level; so hedg'd in
By the Princes infinite Love and Favour to her—

MENIPPUS
She is a handsome Wench.

LEUCIPPE
A delicate, and knows it;
And out of that proof arms her self.

MENIPPUS
Come in then;
I have a great design from the King to you,
And you must work like wax now.

LEUCIPPE
On this Lady?

MENIPPUS
On this, and all your wits call home.

LEUCIPPE
I have done
Toys in my time of some note; old as I am,
I think my brains will work without barm;
Take up the Books.

MENIPPUS
As we go in, I'le tell ye.

[Exeunt.

SCÆNA QUARTA

Enter **ANTIGONUS**, **TIMON**, **LORDS** and a **SOULDIER**.

ANTIGONUS
No face of sorrow for this loss, 'twill choak him,
Nor no man miss a friend, I know his nature
So deep imprest with grief, for what he has suffer'd,
That the least adding to it adds to his ruine;
His loss is not so infinite, I hope, Souldier.

SOULDIER
Faith neither great, nor out of indiscretion.
The young men out of heat.

[Enter **DEMETRIUS**, **LEONTIUS** and **LIEUTENANT**.

ANTIGONUS
I guess the manner.

LORD
The Prince and't like your Grace.

ANTIGONUS
You are welcome home, Sir:
Come, no more sorrow, I have heard your fortune,
And I my self have try'd the like: clear up man,
I will not have ye take it thus; if I doubted
Your fear had lost, and that you had turn'd your back to 'em,
Basely besought their mercies—

LEONTIUS
No, no, by this hand, Sir,
We fought like honest and tall men.

ANTIGONUS
I know't Leontius: or if I thought
Neglect of rule, having his counsel with ye,
Or too vain-glorious appetite of Fame,
Your men forgot and scatter'd.

LEONTIUS
None of these, Sir,
He shew'd himself a noble Gentleman,

Every way apt to rule.

ANTIGONUS
These being granted;
Why should you think you have done an act so hainous,
That nought but discontent dwells round about ye?
I have lost a Battel.

LEONTIUS
I, and fought it hard too.

ANTIGONUS
With as much means as man—

LEONTIUS
Or Devil could urge it.

ANTIGONUS
Twenty to one of our side now.

LEONTIUS
Turn Tables,
Beaten like Dogs again, like Owls, you take it
To heart for flying but a mile before 'em;
And to say the truth, 'twas no flight neither, Sir,
'Twas but a walk, a handsome walk,
I have tumbl'd with this old Body, beaten like a Stock-fish,
And stuck with Arrows, like an arming Quiver,
Blouded and bang'd almost a day before 'em,
And glad I have got off then. Here's a mad Shaver,
He fights his share I am sure, when e'r he comes to't;
Yet I have seen him trip it tithly too,
And cry the Devil take the hindmost ever.

LIEUTENANT
I learnt it of my Betters.

LEONTIUS
Boudge at this?

ANTIGONUS
Has Fortune but one Face?

LIEUTENANT
In her best Vizard
Methinks she looks but lowzily.

ANTIGONUS

Chance, though she faint now,
And sink below our expectations,
Is there no hope left strong enough to buoy her?

DEMETRIUS
'Tis not, this day I fled before the Enemy,
And lost my People, left mine Honour murder'd,
My maiden Honour, never to be ransom'd,
(Which to a noble Soul is too too sensible)
Afflicts me with this sadness; most of these,
Time may turn straight again, experience perfect,
And new Swords cut new ways to nobler Fortunes.
O I have lost—

ANTIGONUS
As you are mine forget it:
I do not think it loss.

DEMETRIUS
O Sir, forgive me,
I have lost my friends, those worthy Souls bred with me,
I have lost my self, they were the pieces of me:
I have lost all Arts, my Schools are taken from me,
Honour and Arms, no emulation left me:
I liv'd to see these men lost, look'd upon it:
These men that twin'd their loves to mine, their vertues;
O shame of shames! I saw and could not save 'em,
This carries Sulphur in't, this burns, and boils me,
And like a fatal Tomb, bestrides my memory.

ANTIGONUS
This was hard fortune, but if alive, and taken,
They shall be ransom'd: let it be at Millions.

DEMETRIUS
They are dead, they are dead.

LIEUTENANT
When wou'd he weep for me thus?
I may be dead and powder'd.

LEONTIUS
Good Prince, grieve not:
We are not certain of their deaths: the Enemy,
Though he be hot, and keen,
Yet holds good Quarter.
What Noise is this?

[Great Shout within: Enter **GENTLEMEN**.

LIEUTENANT
He does not follow us?
Give me a Steeple top.

LEONTIUS
They live, they live, Sir.

ANTIGONUS
Hold up your manly face.
They live, they are here, Son.

DEMETRIUS
These are the men.

1ST GENTLEMAN
They are, and live to honour ye.

DEMETRIUS
How 'scap'd ye noble friends? methought I saw ye
Even in the Jaws of Death.

2ND GENTLEMAN
Thanks to our folly,
That spur'd us on; we were indeed hedg'd round in't;
And ev'n beyond the hand of succour, beaten,
Unhors'd, disarm'd: and what we lookt for then, Sir,
Let such poor weary Souls that hear the Bell knoll,
And see the Grave a digging, tell.

DEMETRIUS
For Heavens sake
Delude mine Eyes no longer! how came ye off?

1ST GENTLEMAN
Against all expectation, the brave Seleucus,
I think this day enamour'd on your Vertue,
When, through the Troops, he saw ye shoot like lightning;
And at your manly courage all took fire;
And after that, the misery we fell to
The never-certain Fate of War, considering,
As we stood all before him, Fortunes ruines,
Nothing but Death expecting, a short time
He made a stand upon our Youths and Fortunes.
Then with an eye of mercy inform'd his Judgment,
How yet unripe we were, unblown, unharden'd,
Unfitted for such fatal ends; he cryed out to us,

Go Gentlemen, commend me to your Master,
To the most High, and Hopeful Prince, Demetrius;
Tell him the Valour that he showed against me
This day, the Virgin Valour, and true fire,
Deserves even from an Enemy this courtesie;
Your Lives, and Arms freely. I'll give 'em: thank him.
And thus we are return'd, Sir.

LEONTIUS
Faith, 'twas well done;
'Twas bravely done; was't not a noble part, Sir?

LIEUTENANT
Had I been there, up had I gone, I am sure on't;
These noble tricks I never durst trust 'em yet.

LEONTIUS
Let me not live, and't were not a famed honesty;
It takes me such a tickling way: now would I wish Heaven,
But e'n the happiness, e'n that poor blessing
For all the sharp afflictions thou hast sent me,
But e'n i'th' head o'th' field, to take Seleucus.
I should do something memorable: fie, sad still?

1ST GENTLEMAN
Do you grieve, we are come off?

DEMETRIUS
Unransom'd, was it?

2ND GENTLEMAN
It was, Sir.

DEMETRIUS
And with such a fame to me?
Said ye not so?

LEONTIUS
Ye have heard it.

DEMETRIUS
O Leontius!
Better I had lost 'em all: my self had perish'd,
And all my Fathers hopes.

LEONTIUS
Mercy upon you;
What ails you, Sir? Death, do not make fools on's,

Neither go to Church, nor tarry at home,
That's a fine Horn-pipe?

ANTIGONUS
What's now your grief, Demetrius?

DEMETRIUS
Did he not beat us twice?

LEONTIUS
He beat, a Pudding;
Beat us but once.

DEMETRIUS
H'as beat me twice, and beat me to a Coward.
Beat me to nothing.

LIEUTENANT
Is not the Devil in him?

LEONTIUS
I pray it be no worse.

DEMETRIUS
Twice conquer'd me.

LEONTIUS
Bear witness all the world, I am a Dunce here.

DEMETRIUS
With valour first he struck me, then with honour,
That stroak Leontius, that stroak, dost thou not feel it?

LEONTIUS
Whereabouts was it? for I remember nothing yet.

DEMETRIUS
All these Gentlemen
That were his Prisoners—

LEONTIUS
Yes, he set 'em free, Sir,
With Arms and honour.

DEMETRIUS
There, there, now thou hast it;
At mine own weapon, Courtesie has beaten me,
At that I was held a Master in, he has cow'd me,

Hotter than all the dint o'th' Fight he has charg'd me:
Am I not now a wretched fellow? think on't;
And when thou hast examin'd all wayes honorable,
And find'st no door left open to requite this,
Conclude I am a wretch, and was twice beaten.

ANTIGONUS
I have observ'd your way, and understand it,
And equal love it as Demetrius,
My noble child thou shalt not fall in vertue,
I and my power will sink first: you Leontius,
Wait for a new Commission, ye shall out again,
And instantly: you shall not lodge this night here,
Not see a friend, nor take a blessing with ye,
Before ye be i'th' field: the enemy is up still,
And still in full design: Charge him again, Son,
And either bring home that again thou hast lost there,
Or leave thy body by him.

DEMETRIUS
Ye raise me,
And now I dare look up again, Leontius.

LEONTIUS
I, I, Sir, I am thinking who we shall take of 'em,
To make all straight; and who we shall give to th' Devil.
What saist thou now Lieutenant?

LIEUTENANT
I say nothing.
Lord what ail I, that I have no mind to fight now?
I find my constitution mightily alter'd
Since I came home: I hate all noises too,
Especially the noise of Drums; I am now as well
As any living man; why not as valiant?
To fight now, is a kind of vomit to me,
It goes against my stomach.

DEMETRIUS
Good Sir, presently;
You cannot doe your Son so fair a favour.

ANTIGONUS
'Tis my intent: I'le see ye march away too.
Come, get your men together presently, Leontius,
And press where please you, as you march.

LEONTIUS

We goe Sir.

ANTIGONUS
Wait you on me, I'le bring ye to your command,
And then to fortune give you up.

DEMETRIUS
Ye love me.

[Exit.

LEONTIUS
Goe, get the Drums, beat round, Lieutenant.

LIEUTENANT
Hark ye, Sir,
I have a foolish business they call marriage.

LEONTIUS
After the wars are done.

LIEUTENANT
The partie staies Sir,
I have giv'n the Priest his mony too: all my friends Sir,
My Father, and my Mother.

LEONTIUS
Will you goe forward?

LIEUTENANT
She brings a pretty matter with her.

LEONTIUS
Half a dozen Bastards.

LIEUTENANT
Some fortie Sir.

LEONTIUS
A goodly competency.

LIEUTENANT
I mean Sir, pounds a year; I'le dispatch the matter,
'Tis but a night or two; I'le overtake ye Sir.

LEONTIUS
The 2 old legions, yes: where lies the horse-quarter?

LIEUTENANT
And if it be a boy, I'le even make bold Sir.

LEONTIUS
Away with your whore,
A plague o' your whore, you damn'd Rogue,
Now ye are cur'd and well; must ye be clicketing?

LIEUTENANT
I have broke my mind to my Ancient, in my absence,
He's a sufficient Gentleman.

LEONTIUS
Get forward.

LIEUTENANT
Only receive her portion.

LEONTIUS
Get ye forward;
Else I'le bang ye forward.

LIEUTENANT
Strange Sir,
A Gentleman and an officer cannot have the liberty
To doe the office of a man.

LEONTIUS
Shame light on thee,
How came this whore into thy head?

LIEUTENANT
This whore Sir?
'Tis strange, a poor whore.

LEONTIUS
Do not answer me,
Troop, Troop away; do not name this whore again,
Or think there is a whore.

LIEUTENANT
That's very hard Sir.

LEONTIUS
For if thou dost, look to't, I'le have thee guelded,
I'le walk ye out before me: not a word more.

[Exeunt.

SCÆNA QUINTA

Enter **LEUCIPPE**, and **GOVERNESS**.

LEUCIPPE
Ye are the Mistris of the house ye say,
Where this young Lady lies.

GOVERNESS
For want of a better.

LEUCIPPE
You may be good enough for such a purpose:
When was the Prince with her? answer me directly.

GOVERNESS
Not since he went a warring.

LEUCIPPE
Very well then:
What carnal copulation are you privie to
Between these two? be not afraid, we are women,
And may talk thus amongst our selves, no harm in't.

GOVERNESS
No sure, there's no harm in't, I conceive that;
But truly, that I ever knew the Gentlewoman
Otherwise given, than a hopefull Gentlewoman—

LEUCIPPE
You'l grant me the Prince loves her?

GOVERNESS
There I am with ye.
And the gods bless her, promises her mightily.

LEUCIPPE
Stay there a while. And gives her gifts?

GOVERNESS
Extreamly;
And truly makes a very Saint of her.

LEUCIPPE
I should think now,

(Good woman let me have your judgement with me,
I see 'tis none of the worst: Come sit down by me)
That these two cannot love so tenderly.

GOVERNESS
Being so young as they are too.

LEUCIPPE
You say well—
But that methinks some further promises—

GOVERNESS
Yes, yes,
I have heard the Prince swear he would marry her.

LEUCIPPE
Very well still: they do not use to fall out?

GOVERNESS
The tenderest Chickens to one another,
They cannot live an hour asunder.

LEUCIPPE
I have done then;
And be you gone; you know your charge, and do it.
You know whose will it is; if you transgress it—
That is, if any have access, or see her,
Before the Kings will be fulfill'd—

GOVERNESS
Not the Prince, Madam?

LEUCIPPE
You'l be hang'd if you doe it, that I'le assure ye.

GOVERNESS
But ne'retheless, I'le make bold to obey ye.

LEUCIPPE
Away, and to your business then.

GOVERNESS
'Tis done, Madam.

[Exeunt.

ACTUS TERTIUS

SCÆNA PRIMA

Enter **ANTIGONUS** and **MENIPPUS**.

ANTIGONUS
Thou hast taken wondrous pains; but yet Menippus,
You understand not of what bloud and country.

MENIPPUS
I labour'd that, but cannot come to know it.
A Greek I am sure she is, she speaks this language.

ANTIGONUS
Is she so excellent handsom?

MENIPPUS
Most inticing.

ANTIGONUS
Sold for a prisoner?

MENIPPUS
Yes Sir,
Some poor creature.

ANTIGONUS
And he loves tenderly?

MENIPPUS
They say extreamly.

ANTIGONUS
'Tis well prevented then: yes, I perceiv'd it:
When he took leave now, he made a hundred stops,
Desir'd an hour, but half an hour, a minute,
Which I with anger cross'd; I knew his business,
I knew 'twas she he hunted on; this journey, man,
I beat out suddenly for her cause intended,
And would not give him time to breath. When comes she?

MENIPPUS
This morning Sir.

ANTIGONUS
Lodge her to all delight then:
For I would have her try'd to th' test: I know,

She must be some crackt coyn, not fit his traffique, (her,
Which when we have found, the shame will make him leave
Or we shall work a nearer way: I'le bury him,
And with him all the hopes I have cast upon him,
E're he shall dig his own grave in that woman:
You know which way to bring her: I'le stand close there,
To view her as she passes: and do you hear Menippus,
Observe her with all sweetness: humour her,
'Twill make her lie more careless to our purposes.
Away, and take what helps you please.

MENIPPUS
I am gone Sir.

[Exeunt.

SCÆNA SECUNDA

Enter **CELIA** and **GOVERNESS**.

CELIA
Governess, from whom was this Gown sent me?
Prethee be serious true; I will not wear't else:
'Tis a handsom one.

GOVERNESS
As though you know not?

CELIA
No faith:
But I believe, for certain too, yet I wonder,
Because it was his caution, this poor way,
Still to preserve me from the curious searchings
Of greedy eyes.

GOVERNESS
You have it: does it please you?

CELIA
'Tis very rich, methinks too, prethee tell me?

GOVERNESS
From one that likes you well, never look coy, Lady;
These are no gifts, to be put off with powtings.

CELIA

Powtings, and gifts? is it from any stranger?

GOVERNESS
You are so curious, that there is no talk to ye.
What if it be I pray ye?

CELIA
Unpin good Governess,
Quick, quick.

GOVERNESS
Why, what's the matter?

CELIA
Quick, good Governess:
Fie on't, how beastly it becomes me! poorly!
A trick put in upon me? well said Governess:
I vow I would not wear it—out, it smells musty.
Are these your tricks? now I begin to smell it,
Abominable musty; will you help me?
The Prince will come again—

GOVERNESS
You are not mad sure?

CELIA
As I live I'le cut it off: a pox upon it;
For sure it was made for that use; do you bring me Liveries?
Stales to catch Kites? dost thou laugh too, thou base woman?

GOVERNESS
I cannot chuse, if I should be hang'd.

CELIA
Abuse me,
And then laugh at me too?

GOVERNESS
I do not abuse ye:
Is it abuse, to give him drink that's thirsty?
You want cloaths; is it such a hainous sin I beseech ye,
To see you stor'd?

CELIA
There is no greater wickedness
Than this way.

GOVERNESS

What way?

CELIA
I shall curse thee fearfully,
If thou provok'st me further: and take heed, woman;
My curses never miss.

GOVERNESS
Curse him that sent it.

CELIA
Tell but his name—

GOVERNESS
You dare not curse him.

CELIA
Dare not?
By this fair light—

GOVERNESS
You are so full of passion—

CELIA
Dare not be good? be honest? dare not curse him?

GOVERNESS
I think you dare not: I believe so.

CELIA
Speak him.

GOVERNESS
Up with your valour then, up with it bravely,
And take your full charge.

CELIA
If I do not, hang me;
Tell but his name.

GOVERNESS
'Twas Prince Demetrius sent it:
Now, now, give fire, kill him i'th' eye now Lady.

CELIA
Is he come home?

GOVERNESS

It seems so; but your curse now.

CELIA
You do not lie, I hope.

GOVERNESS
You dare not curse him.

CELIA
Prethee do not abuse me: is he come home indeed?
For I would now with all my heart believe thee.

GOVERNESS
Nay, you may chuse: alas, I deal for strangers,
That send ye scurvie musty Gowns, stale Liveries:
I have my tricks.

CELIA
'Tis a good gown, a handsome one;
I did but jest; where is he?

GOVERNESS
He that sent it—

CELIA
How? he that sent it? is't come to that again?
Thou canst not be so foolish: prethee speak out,
I may mistake thee.

GOVERNESS
I said he that sent it.

CELIA
Curse o' my life: why dost thou vex me thus?
I know thou meanest Demetrius, dost thou not?
I charge thee speak truth: if it be any other,
Thou knowst the charge he gave thee, and the justice
His anger will'inflift, if e're he know this,
As know he shall, he shall, thou spightfull woman,
Thou beastly woman; and thou shalt know too late too,
And feel too sensible, I am no ward,
No sale stuff for your money Merchants that sent if?
Who dare send me, or how durst thou, thou—

GOVERNESS
What you please:
For this is ever the reward of service.
The Prince shall bring the next himself.

CELIA
'Tis strange
That you should deal so peevishly: beshrew ye,
You have put me in a heat.

GOVERNESS
I am sure ye have kill'd me:
I ne're receiv'd such language: I can but wait upon ye,
And be your drudge; keep a poor life to serve ye.

CELIA
You know my nature is too easie, Governess,
And you know now, I am sorry too: how does he?

GOVERNESS
O God, my head.

CELIA
Prethee be well, and tell me,
Did he speak of me, since he came? nay, see now,
If thou wilt leave this tyranny? good sweet governess,
Did he but name his Celia? look upon me,
Upon my faith I meant no harm: here, take this,
And buy thy self some trifles: did he good wench?

GOVERNESS
He loves ye but too dearly.

CELIA
That's my good Governess.

GOVERNESS
There's more cloaths making for ye.

CELIA
More cloaths?

GOVERNESS
More:
Richer and braver; I can tell ye that news;
And twenty glorious things.

CELIA
To what use Sirrah?

GOVERNESS
Ye are too good for our house now: we poor wretches

Shall lose the comfort of ye.

CELIA
No, I hope not.

GOVERNESS
For ever lose ye Lady.

CELIA
Lose me? wherefore?
I hear of no such thing.

GOVERNESS
'Tis sure it must be so:
You must shine now at Court: such preparation,
Such hurry, and such hanging rooms—

CELIA
To th' Court wench?
Was it to th' Court thou saidst?

GOVERNESS
You'l find it so.

CELIA
Stay, stay, this cannot be.

GOVERNESS
I say it must be:
I hope to find ye still the same good Lady.

CELIA
To th' Court? this stumbles me: art sure for me wench,
This preparation is?

GOVERNESS
She is perilous crafty:
I fear too honest for us all too. Am I sure I live?

CELIA
To th' Court? this cannot down: what should I do there?
Why should he on a suddain change his mind thus,
And not make me acquainted? sure he loves me;
His vow was made against it, and mine with him:
At least while this King liv'd: he will come hither,
And see me e're I goe?

GOVERNESS

Wou'd some wise woman
Had her in working. That I think he will not,
Because he means with all joy there to meet ye.
Ye shall hear more within this hour.

CELIA
A Courtier?
What may that meaning be? sure he will see me
If he be come, he must: Hark ye good Governess,
What age is the King of?

GOVERNESS
He's an old man, and full of business.

CELIA
I fear too full indeed: what Ladys are there?
I would be loth to want good company.

GOVERNESS
Delicate young Ladys, as you would desire;
And when you are acquainted, the best company.

CELIA
'Tis very well: prethee goe in, let's talk more.
For though I fear a trick, Fie bravely try it.

GOVERNESS
I see he must be cunning,
Knocks this Doe down.

[Exeunt.

SCÆNA TERTIA

Enter **LIEUTENANT** and **LEONTIUS**. Drums within.

LEONTIUS
You shall not have your will, sirrah, are ye running?
Have ye gotten a toy in your heels? Is this a season,
When honour pricks ye on, to prick your ears up,
After your whore, your Hobby-horse?

LIEUTENANT
Why look ye now:
What a strange man are you? would you have a man fight
At all hours all alike?

LEONTIUS
Do but fight something;
But half a blow, and put thy stomach to't:
Turn but thy face, and do-make mouths at 'em.

LIEUTENANT
And have my teeth knockt out; I thank ye heartily,
Ye are my dear friend.

LEONTIUS
What a devil ails thee?
Dost long to be hang'd?

LIEUTENANT
Faith Sir, I make no suit for't:
But rather Fhan I would live thus out of charity,
Continually in brawling—

LEONTIUS
Art thou not he?
I may be cosen'd—

LIEUTENANT
I shall be discover'd.

LEONTIUS
That in the midst of thy most hellish pains,
When thou wert crawling sick, didst aim at wonders,
When thou wert mad with pain?

LIEUTENANT
Ye have found the cause out;
I had ne're been mad to fight else: I confess Sir,
The daily torture of my side that vext me,
Made me as daily careless what became of me,
Till a kind sword there wounded me, and eas'd me;
'Twas nothing in my valour fought; I am well now,
And take some pleasure in my life, methinks now,
It shews as mad a thing to me to see you scuffle,
And kill one another foolishly for honour,
As 'twas to you, to see me play the coxcomb.

LEONTIUS
And wilt thou ne're fight more?

LIEUTENANT
I'th' mind I am in.

LEONTIUS
Nor never be sick again?

LIEUTENANT
I hope I shall not.

LEONTIUS
Prethee be sick again: prethee, I beseech thee,
Be just so sick again.

LIEUTENANT
I'le just be hang'd first.

LEONTIUS
If all the Arts that are can make a Colique,
Therefore look to't: or if imposthumes, mark me,
As big as foot-balls—

LIEUTENANT
Deliver me.

LEONTIUS
Or stones of ten pound weight i'th' kidneys,
Through ease and ugly dyets may be gather'd;
I'le feed ye up my self Sir, I'le prepare ye,
You cannot fight, unless the Devil tear ye,
You shall not want provocations, I'le scratch ye,
I'le have thee have the tooth-ach, and the head-ach.

LIEUTENANT
Good Colonel, I'le doe any thing.

LEONTIUS
No, no, nothing—
Then will I have thee blown with a pair of Smiths bellows,
Because ye shall be sure to have a round gale with ye,
Fill'd full of oyle o'Devil, and Aqua-fortis,
And let these work, these may provoke.

LIEUTENANT
Good Colonel.

LEONTIUS
A coward in full bloud; prethee be plain with me,
Will roasting doe thee any good?

LIEUTENANT

Nor basting neither, Sir.

LEONTIUS
Marry that goes hard.

[Enter **1ST GENTLEMAN**.

1ST GENTLEMAN
Where are you Colonel?
The Prince experts ye Sir; h'as hedg'd the enemy
Within a streight, where all the hopes and valours
Of all men living cannot force a passage,
He has 'em now.

LEONTIUS
I knew all this before Sir,
I chalk'd him out his way: but do you see that thing there?

LIEUTENANT
Nay good sweet Colonel, I'le fight a little.

LEONTIUS
That thing?

1ST GENTLEMAN
What thing? I see the brave Lieutenant.

LEONTIUS
Rogue, what a name hast thou lost?

LIEUTENANT
You may help it,
Yet you may help't: I'le doe ye any courtesie:
I know you love a wench well.

[Enter **2ND GENTLEMAN**.

LEONTIUS
Look upon him;
Do you look too.

2ND GENTLEMAN
What should I look on?
I come to tell ye, the Prince stayes your direction,
We have 'em now i'th' Coop, Sir.

LEONTIUS
Let 'em rest there,

And chew upon their miseries: but look first—

LIEUTENANT
I cannot fight for all this.

LEONTIUS
Look on this fellow.

2ND GENTLEMAN
I know him; 'tis the valiant brave Lieutenant.

LEONTIUS
Canst thou hear this, and play the Rogue? steal off quickly,
Behind me quickly neatly do it,
And rush into the thickest of the enemy,
And if thou kill'st but two.

LIEUTENANT
You may excuse me,
'Tis not my fault: I dare not fight.

LEONTIUS
Be rul'd yet,
I'le beat thee on; goe wink and fight: a plague upon your sheeps heart.

2ND GENTLEMAN
What's all this matter?

1ST GENTLEMAN
Nay I cannot shew ye.

LEONTIUS
Here's twenty pound, goe but smell to 'em.

LIEUTENANT
Alas Sir,
I have taken such a cold I can smell nothing.

LEONTIUS
I can smell a Rascal, a rank Rascal:
Fye, how he stinks, stinks like a tyred Jade.

2ND GENTLEMAN
What Sir?

LEONTIUS
Why, that Sir, do not you smell him?

2ND GENTLEMAN
Smell him?

LIEUTENANT
I must endure.

LEONTIUS
Stinks like a dead Dog, Carrion—
There's no such damnable smell under Heaven,
As the faint sweat of a Coward: will ye fight yet?

LIEUTENANT
Nay, now I defie ye; ye have spoke the worst ye can
Of me, and if every man should take what you say
To the heart.—

LEONTIUS
God ha' Mercy,
God ha' Mercy with all my heart; here I forgive thee;
And fight, or fight not, do but goe along with us,
And keep my Dog.

LIEUTENANT
I love a good Dog naturally.

1ST GENTLEMAN
What's all this stir, Lieutenant?

LIEUTENANT
Nothing Sir,
But a slight matter of argument.

LEONTIUS
Pox take thee.
Sure I shall love this Rogue, he's so pretty a Coward.
Come Gentlemen, let's up now, and if fortune
Dare play the slut again, I'le never more Saint her,
Come play-fellow, come, prethee come up; come chicken,
I have a way shall fit yet: A tame knave,
Come, look upon us.

LIEUTENANT
I'le tell ye who does best boyes.

[Exeunt.

SCÆNA QUARTO

Enter **ANTIGONUS** and **MENIPPUS**, above.

MENIPPUS
I saw her coming out.

ANTIGONUS
Who waits upon her?

MENIPPUS
Timon, Charinthus, and some other Gentlemen,
By me appointed.

ANTIGONUS
Where's your wife?

MENIPPUS
She's ready
To entertain her here Sir; and some Ladies
Fit for her lodgings.

ANTIGONUS
How shews she in her trim now?

MENIPPUS
Oh most divinely sweet.

ANTIGONUS
Prethee speak softly.
How does she take her coming?

MENIPPUS
She bears it bravely;
But what she thinks—For Heaven sake Sir preserve me—
If the Prince chance to find this.

ANTIGONUS
Peace ye old fool;
She thinks to meet him here.

MENIPPUS
That's all the Project.

ANTIGONUS
Was she hard to bring?

MENIPPUS

No she believ'd it quickly,
And quickly made her self fit, the Gown a little,
And those new things she has not been acquainted with,
At least in this place, where she liv'd a prisoner,
Troubled and stirr'd her mind. But believe me Sir,
She has worn as good, they sit so apted to her;
And she is so great a Mistris of disposure:
Here they come now: but take a full view of her.

[Enter **CELIA**, **TIMON**, **CHARINTHUS** and **GENTLEMAN**.

ANTIGONUS
How cheerfully she looks? how she salutes all?
And how she views the place? she is very young sure:
That was an admirable smile, a catching one,
The very twang of Cupids bow sung in it:
She has two-edg'd eyes, they kill o' both sides.

MENIPPUS
She makes a stand, as though she would speak.

ANTIGONUS
Be still then.

CELIA
Good Gentlemen, trouble your selves no further,
I had thought sure to have met a noble friend here.

TIMON
Ye may meet many Lady.

CELIA
Such as you are
I covet few or none, Sir.

CHARINTHUS
Will you walk this way,
And take the sweets o'th' garden? cool and close, Lady.

CELIA
Methinks this open air's far better, tend ye that way
Pray where's the woman came along?

CHARINTHUS
What woman?

CELIA
The woman of the house I lay at.

TIMON
Woman?
Here was none came along sure.

CELIA
Sure I am catcht then:
Pray where's the Prince?

CHARINTHUS
He will not be long from ye,
We are his humble Servants.

CELIA
I could laugh now,
To see how finely I am cozen'd: yet I fear not,
For sure I know a way to scape all dangers.

TIMON
Madam, your lodgings lye this way.

CELIA
My Lodgings?
For Heaven sake Sir, what office do I bear here?

TIMON
The great commander of all hearts.

[Enter **LEUCIPPE** and **LADIES**.

CELIA
You have hit it.
I thank your sweet heart for it. Who are these now?

CHARINTHUS
Ladies that come to serve ye.

CELIA
Well consider'd,
Are you my Servants?

LADY
Servants to your pleasures.

CELIA
I dare believe ye, but I dare not trust ye:
Catch'd with a trick? well, I must bear it patiently:
Methinks this Court's a neat place: all the people

Of so refin'd a size—

TIMON
This is no poor Rogue.

LEUCIPPE
Were it a Paradise to please your fancy,
And entertain the sweetness you bring with ye.

CELIA
Take breath;
You are fat, and many words may melt ye,
This is three Bawdes beaten into one; bless me Heaven,
What shall become of me? I am i'th' pitfall:
O' my conscience, this is the old viper, and all these little ones
Creep every night into her belly; do you hear plump servant
And you my little sucking Ladies, you must teach me,
For I know you are excellent at carriage,
How to behave my self, for I am rude yet:
But you say the Prince will come?

LADY
Will flie to see you.

CELIA
For look you if a great man, say the King now
Should come and visit me?

MENIPPUS
She names ye.

ANTIGONUS
Peace fool.

CELIA
And offer me a kindness, such a kindness.

LEUCIPPE
I, such a kindness.

CELIA
True Lady such a kindness,
What shall that kindness be now?

LEUCIPPE
A witty Lady,
Learn little ones, learn.

CELIA
Say it be all his favour.

LEUCIPPE
And a sweet saying 'tis.

CELIA
And I grow peevish?

LEUCIPPE
You must not be negleftfull.

CELIA
There's the matter,
There's the main doctrine now, and I may miss it,
Or a kind handsom Gentleman?

LEUCIPPE
You say well.

CELIA
They'l count us basely bred.

LEUCIPPE
Not freely nurtur'd.

CELIA
I'le take thy counsel.

LEUCIPPE
'Tis an excellent woman.

CELIA
I find a notable volum here, a learned one;
Which way? for I would fain be in my chamber;
In truth sweet Ladies, I grow weary; fie,
How hot the air beats on me!

LADY
This way Madam.

CELIA
Now by mine honour, I grow wondrous faint too.

LEUCIPPE
Your fans sweet Gentlewomen, your fans.

CELIA

Since I am fool'd,
I'le make my self some sport, though I pay dear for't.

[Exit.

MENIPPUS
You see now what a manner of woman she is Sir.

ANTIGONUS
Thou art an ass.

MENIPPUS
Is this a fit love for the Prince:

ANTIGONUS
A coxcombe:
Now by my crown a daintie wench, a sharp wench,
And/a matchless Spirit: how she jeer'd 'em?
How carelesly she scoff'd 'em? use her nobly;
I would I had not seen her: wait anon,
And then you shall have more to trade upon.

[Exeunt.

SCÆNA QUINTA

Enter **LEONTIUS** and the **2ND GENTLEMAN**.

LEONTIUS
We must keep a round, and a strong watch to night,
The Prince will not charge the Enemy till the morning:
But for the trick I told ye for this Rascal,
This rogue, that health and strong heart makes a coward.

2ND GENTLEMAN
I, if it take.

LEONTIUS
Ne're fear it, the Prince has it,
And if he let it fall, I must not know it;
He will suspecl: me presently: but you two
May help the plough.

2ND GENTLEMAN
That he is sick again.

LEONTIUS
Extreamly sick: his disease grown incurable,
Never yet found, nor touch'd at.

[Enter **LIEUTENANT**.

2ND GENTLEMAN
Well, we have it,
And here he comes.

LEONTIUS
The Prince has been upon him,
What a flatten face he has now? it takes, believe it;
How like an Ass he looks?

LIEUTENANT
I feel no great pain,
At least, I think I do not; yet I feel sensibly
I grow extreamly faint: how cold I sweat now!

LEONTIUS
So, so, so.

LIEUTENANT
And now 'tis ev'n too true, I feel a pricking,
A pricking, a strange pricking: how it tingles!
And as it were a stitch too: the Prince told me,
And every one cri'd out I was a dead man;
I had thought I had been as well—

LEONTIUS
Upon him now Boys,
And do it most demurely.

1ST GENTLEMAN
How now Lieutenant?

LIEUTENANT
I thank ye Gentlemen.

1ST GENTLEMAN
'Life, how looks this man?
How dost thou good Lieutenant?

2ND GENTLEMAN
I ever told ye
This man was never cur'd, I see it too plain now;
How do you feel your self? you look not perfect,

How dull his eye hangs?

1ST GENTLEMAN
That may be discontent.

2ND GENTLEMAN
Believe me friend, I would not suffer now
The tith of those pains this man feels; mark his forehead
What a cloud of cold dew hangs upon't?

LIEUTENANT
I have it,
Again I have it; how it grows upon me!
A miserable man I am.

LEONTIUS
Ha, ha, ha,
A miserable man thou shall be,
This is the tamest Trout I ever tickl'd.

[Enter **TWO PHYSICIANS**.

1ST PHYSICIAN
This way he went.

2ND PHYSICIAN
Pray Heaven we find him living,
He's a brave fellow, 'tis pity he should perish thus.

1ST PHYSICIAN
A strong hearted man, and of a notable sufferance.

LIEUTENANT
Oh, oh.

1ST GENTLEMAN
How now? how is it man?

LIEUTENANT
Oh Gentlemen,
Never so full of pain.

2ND GENTLEMAN
Did I not tell ye?

LIEUTENANT
Never so full of pain, Gentlemen.

1ST PHYSICIAN
He is here;
How do you, Sir?

2ND PHYSICIAN
Be of good comfort, Souldier,
The Prince has sent us to you.

LIEUTENANT
Do you think I may live?

2ND PHYSICIAN
He alters hourly, strangely.

1ST PHYSICIAN
Yes, you may live: but—

LEONTIUS
Finely butted, Doctor.

1ST GENTLEMAN
Do not discourage him.

1ST PHYSICIAN
He must be told truth,
'Tis now too late to trifle.

[Enter **DEMETRIUS** and **GENTLEMAN**.

2ND GENTLEMAN
Here the Prince comes.

DEMETRIUS
How now Gentlemen?

2ND GENTLEMAN
Bewailing, Sir, a Souldier,
And one I think, your Grace will grieve to part with,
But every living thing—

DEMETRIUS
'Tis true, must perish,
Our lives are but our marches to our graves,
How dost thou now Lieutenant?

LIEUTENANT
Faith 'tis true, Sir,
We are but spans, and Candles ends.

LEONTIUS
He's finely mortified.

DEMETRIUS
Thou art heart whole yet I see he alters strangely,
And that apace too; I saw it this morning in him,
When he poor man, I dare swear—

LIEUTENANT
No believ't, Sir,
I never felt it.

DEMETRIUS
Here lies the pain now: how he is swel'd?

1ST PHYSICIAN
The Impostume
Fed with a new malignant humour now,
Will grow to such a bigness, 'tis incredible,
The compass of a Bushel will not hold it.
And with such a Hell of torture it will rise too—

DEMETRIUS
Can you endure me touch it?

LIEUTENANT
Oh, I beseech you, Sir:
I feel you sensibly ere you come near me.

DEMETRIUS
He's finely wrought, he must be cut, no Cure else,
And suddenly, you see how fast he blows out.

LIEUTENANT
Good Master Doctors, let me be beholding to you,
I feel I cannot last.

2ND PHYSICIAN
For what Lieutenant?

LIEUTENANT
But ev'n for half a dozen Cans of good Wine,
That I may drink my will out: I faint hideously. (men,

DEMETRIUS
Fetch him some Wine; and since he must go Gentle—Why
let him take his journey merrily.

[Enter **SERVANT** with Wine.

LIEUTENANT
That's ev'n the nearest way.

LEONTIUS
I could laugh dead now.

DEMETRIUS
Here, off with that.

LIEUTENANT
These two I give your Grace,
A poor remembrance of a dying man, Sir,
And I beseech you wear 'em out.

DEMETRIUS
I will Souldier,
These are fine Legacies.

LIEUTENANT
Among the Gentlemen,
Even all I have left; I am a poor man, naked,
Yet something for remembrance: four a piece Gentlemen,
And so my body where you please.

LEONTIUS
It will work.

LIEUTENANT
I make your Grace my Executor, and I beseech ye
See my poor Will fulfill'd: sure I shall walk else.

DEMETRIUS
As full as they can be fill'd, here's my hand, Souldier.

1ST GENTLEMAN
The Wine will tickle him.

LIEUTENANT
I would hear a Drum beat,
But to see how I could endure it.

DEMETRIUS
Beat a Drum there.

[Drum within.

LIEUTENANT
Oh Heavenly Musick, I would hear one sing to't;
I am very full of pain.

DEMETRIUS
Sing? 'tis impossible.

LIEUTENANT
Why, then I would drink a Drum full:
Where lies the Enemy?

2ND GENTLEMAN
Why, here close by.

LEONTIUS
Now he begins to muster.

LIEUTENANT
And dare he fight?
Dare he fight Gentlemen?

1ST PHYSICIAN
You must not cut him:
He's gone then in a moment; all the hope left, is
To work his weakness into suddain anger,
And make him raise his passion above his pain,
And so dispose him on the Enemy;
His body then, being stir'd with violence,
Will purge it self and break the sore.

DEMETRIUS
'Tis true, Sir.

1ST PHYSICIAN
And then my life for his.

LIEUTENANT
I will not dye thus.

DEMETRIUS
But he is too weak to do—

LIEUTENANT
Dye like a Dog?

2ND PHYSICIAN
I, he's weak, but yet he's heart whole.

LIEUTENANT
Hem.

DEMETRIUS
An excellent sign.

LIEUTENANT
Hem.

DEMETRIUS
Stronger still, and better.

LIEUTENANT
Hem, hem; ran, tan, tan, tan, tan.

[Exit.

1ST PHYSICIAN
Now he's i'th' way on't.

DEMETRIUS
Well go thy waies, thou wilt do something certain.

LEONTIUS
And some brave thing, or let mine ears be cut off.
He's finely wrought.

DEMETRIUS
Let's after him.

LEONTIUS
I pray, Sir;
But how this Rogue, when this cloud's melted in him,
And all discover'd—

DEMETRIUS
That's for an after mirth, away, away, away.

[Exit.

SCÆNA SEXTA

Enter **SELECIUS**, **LYSIMACHUS**, **PTOLOMIE**, **SOULDIERS**.

SELECIUS

Let no man fear to dye: we love to sleep all,
And death is but the sounder sleep; all ages,
And all hours call us; 'tis so common, easie,
That little Children tread those paths before us;
We are not sick, nor our souls prest with sorrows,
Nor go we out like tedious tales, forgotten;
High, high we come, and hearty to our Funerals,
And as the Sun that sets, in bloud let's fall.

LYSIMACHUS
'Tis true, they have us fast, we cannot scape 'em
Nor keeps the brow of fortune one smile for us,
Dishonourable ends we can scape though,
And (worse than those Captivities) we can die,
And dying nobly, though we leave behind us
These clods of flesh, that are too massie burthens,
Our living souls flie crown'd with living conquests.

PTOLOMIE
They have begun, fight bravely, and fall bravely;
And may that man that seeks to save his life now
By price, or promise, or by fear falls from us,
Never again be blest with name of Souldier.

[Enter a **SOULDIER**.

SELECIUS
How now? who charged first? I seek a brave hand
To set me off in death.

SOULDIER
We are not charg'd, Sir,
The Prince lies still.

SELECIUS
How comes this Larum up then?

SOULDIER
There is one desperate fellow, with the Devil in him
(He never durst do this else) has broke into us,
And here he bangs ye two or three before him,
There five or six; ventures upon whole Companies.

PTOLOMIE
And is not seconded?

SOULDIER
Not a man follows.

SELECIUS
Nor cut i' pieces?

SOULDIER
Their wonder yet has staid 'em.

SELECIUS
Let's in, and see this miracle?

PTOLOMIE
I admire it.

[Exit.

[Enter **LEONTIUS** and **GENTLEMAN**.

LEONTIUS
Fetch him off, fetch him off; I am sure he's clouted;
Did I hot tell you how 'twould take?

1ST GENTLEMAN
'Tis admirable.

[Enter **LIEUTENANT** with Colours in his hand, pursuing **3** or **4 SOULDIERS**.

LIEUTENANT
Follow that blow, my friend, there's at your coxcombs,
I fight to save me from the Surgions miseries.

LEONTIUS
How the Knave curries 'em?

LIEUTENANT
You cannot Rogues,
Till you have my Diseases, flie my fury,
Ye Bread and Butter Rogues, do ye run from me?
And my side would give me leave, I would so hunt ye,
Ye Porridg gutted Slaves, ye Veal broth-Boobies.

[Enter **DEMETRIUS** and **PHYSICIANS** and **GENTLEMEN**.

LEONTIUS
Enough, enough Lieutenant, thou hast done bravely.

DEMETRIUS
Mirrour of man.

LIEUTENANT
There's a Flag for ye, Sir,
I took it out o'th' shop, and never paid for't,
I'le to 'em again, I am not come to th' text yet.

DEMETRIUS
No more my Souldier: beshrew my heart he is hurt sore.

LEONTIUS
Hang him, he'l lick all th^se whole.

1ST PHYSICIAN
Now will we take him,
And Cure him in a trice.

DEMETRIUS
Be careful of him.

LIEUTENANT
Let me live but two years,
And do what ye will with me;
I never had but two hours yet of happiness;
Pray ye give me nothing to provoke my valour,
For I am ev'n as weary of this fighting—

2ND PHYSICIAN
Ye shall have nothing; come to the Princes Tent
And there the Surgions presently shall search ye,
Then to your rest.

LIEUTENANT
A little handsome Litter
To lay me in, and I shall sleep.

LEONTIUS
Look to him.

DEMETRIUS
I do believe a Horse begot this fellow,
He never knew his strength yet; they are our own.

LEONTIUS
I think so, I am cozen'd else; I would but see now
A way to fetch these off, and save their honours.

DEMETRIUS
Only their lives.

LEONTIUS
Pray ye take no way of peace now,
Unless it be with infinite advantage.

DEMETRIUS
I shall be rul'd;
Let the Battels now move forward,
Our self will give the signal:

[Enter Trumpet and **HERALD**.

Now Herald, what's your message?

HERALD
From my Masters,
This honourable courtesie, a Parley
For half an hour, no more, Sir.

DEMETRIUS
Let 'em come on,
They have my Princely word.

[Enter **SELEUCUS, LYSIMACUS, PTOLOMIE, ATTENDANTS, SOULDIERS.**

HERALD
They are here to attend ye.

DEMETRIUS
Now Princes, your demands?

SELECIUS
Peace, if it may be
Without the too much tainture of our honour:
Peace, and we'l buy it too.

DEMETRIUS
At what price?

LYSIMACHUS
Tribute.

PTOLOMIE
At all the charge of this War.

LEONTIUS
That will not do.

SELECIUS

Leontius, you and I have serv'd together,
And run through many a Fortune with our swords,
Brothers in Wounds and Health; one meat has fed us,
One Tent a thousand times from cold night cover'd us:
Our loves have been but one; and had we died then,
One Monument had held our names, and actions:
Why do you set upon your friends such prices?
And sacrifice to giddy chance such Trophies?
Have we forgot to dye? or are our vertues
Less in afflictions constant, than our fortunes?
Ye are deceiv'd old Souldier.

LEONTIUS
I know your worths,
And thus low bow in reverence to your vertues:
Were these my Wars, or led my power in chief here,
I knew then how to meet your memories:
They are my Kings imployments; this man fights now,
To whom I ow all duty, faith, and service;
This man that fled before ye; call back that,
That bloudy day again, call that disgrace home,
And then an easie Peace may sheath our Swords up.
I am not greedy of your lives and fortunes,
Nor do I gape ungratefully to swallow ye.
Honour, the spur of all illustrious natures,
That made you famous Souldiers, and next Kings,
And not ambitious envy strikes me forward.
Will ye unarm, and yield your selves his prisoners?

SELECIUS
We never knew what that sound meant: no Gyves
Shall ever bind this body, but embraces;
Nor weight of sorrow here, till Earth fall on me.

LEONTIUS
Expect our charge then.

LYSIMACHUS
'Tis the nobler courtesie:
And so we leave the hand of Heaven to bless us.

DEMETRIUS
Stay, have you any hope?

SELECIUS
We have none left us,
But that one comfort of our deaths together;
Give us but room to fight.

LEONTIUS
Win it, and wear it.

PTOLOMIE
Call from the hills those Companies hang o're us,
Like bursting Clouds; and then break in, and take us.

DEMETRIUS
Find such a Souldier will forsake advantage,
And we'll draw off to shew I dare be noble,
And hang a light out to ye in this darkness,
The light of peace; give up those Cities, Forts,
And all those Frontier Countries to our uses.

SELECIUS
Is this the Peace? Traitors to those that feed us,
Our Gods and people? give our Countries from us?

LYSIMACHUS
Begin the Knell, it sounds a great deal sweeter.

PTOLOMIE
Let loose your servant, death.

SELECIUS
Fall fate upon us,
Our memories shall never stink behind us.

DEMETRIUS
Seleucus, great Seleucus.

SOULDIER
The Prince calls, Sir.

DEMETRIUS
Thou stock of nobleness, and courtesie,
Thou Father of the War—

LEONTIUS
What means the Prince now?

DEMETRIUS
Give me my Standard here.

LYSIMACHUS
His anger's melted.

DEMETRIUS
You Gentlemen that were his prisoners,
And felt the bounty of that noble nature,
Lay all your hands, and bear these Colours to him,
The Standard of the Kingdom; take it Souldier.

PTOLOMIE
What will this mean?

DEMETRIUS
Thou hast won it, bear it off,
And draw thy men home whilest we wait upon thee.

SELECIUS
You shall have all our Countries.

LYSIMACHUS & PTOLOMIE
All by Heaven, Sir.

DEMETRIUS
I will not have a stone, a bush, a bramble,
No, in the way of courtesie, I'le start ye;
Draw off, and make a lane through all the Army,
That these that have subdu'd us, may march through us.

SELECIUS
Sir, do not make me surfeit with such goodness,
I'le bear your Standard for ye; follow ye.

DEMETRIUS
I swear it shall be so, march through me fairly,
And thine be this days honour, great Seleucus.

PTOLOMIE
Mirrour of noble minds.

DEMETRIUS
Nay then ye hate me.

LEONTIUS
I cannot speak now:

[Exit with Drums, and Shouts.

Well, go thy wayes; at a sure piece of bravery
Thou art the best, these men are won by th' necks now:
I'le send a Post away.

ACTUS QUARTUS

SCÆNA PRIMA

Enter **ANTIGONUS** and **MENIPPUS**.

ANTIGONUS
No aptness in her?

MENIPPUS
Not an immodest motion,
And yet when she is courted,
Makes as wild witty answers.

ANTIGONUS
This more fires me,
I must not have her thus.

MENIPPUS
We cannot alter her.

ANTIGONUS
Have ye put the youths upon her?

MENIPPUS
All that know any thing,
And have been studied how to catch a beauty,
But like so many whelps about an Elephant—
The Prince is coming home, Sir.

ANTIGONUS
I hear that too,
But that's no matter; am I alter'd well?

MENIPPUS
Not to be known I think, Sir.

ANTIGONUS
I must see her.

[Enter **TWO GENTLEMEN** or **LORDS**.

1ST GENTLEMAN
I offered all I had, all I could think of,
I tri'd her through all the points o'th' compass, I think.

2ND GENTLEMAN
She studies to undo the Court, to plant here
The Enemy to our Age, Chastity;
She is the first, that e're bauk'd a close Arbour,
And the sweet contents within: She hates curl'd heads too,
And setting up of beards she swears is Idolatry.

1ST GENTLEMAN
I never knew so fair a face so froze;
Yet she would make one think—

2ND GENTLEMAN
True by her carriage,
For she's as wanton as a Kid to th' out side,
As full of Mocks and Taunts: I kiss'd her hand too,
Walkt with her half an hour.

1ST GENTLEMAN
She heard me sing,
And sung her self too; she sings admirably;
But still when any hope was, as 'tis her trick
To minister enough of those, then presently
With some new flam or other, nothing to the matter,
And such a frown, as would sink all before her,
She takes her Chamber; come, we shall not be the last fools.

2ND GENTLEMAN
Not by a hundred I hope; 'tis a strange wench.

ANTIGONUS
This screws me up still higher.

[Enter **CELIA** and **LADIES** behind her.

MENIPPUS
Here she comes, Sir.

ANTIGONUS
Then be you gone; and take the Women with ye,
And lay those Jewels in her way.

CELIA
If I stay longer
I shall number as many Lovers as Lais did;
How they flock after me! upon my Conscience,
I have had a dozen Horses given me this morning,
I'le ev'n set up a Troop, and turn She-souldier,
A good discreet wench now, that were not hidebound

Might raise a fine estate here, and suddenly:
For these warm things will give their Souls—I can go no where
Without a world of offerings to my Excellence:
I am a Queen, a Goddesse, I know not what—
And no constellation in all Heaven, but I out-shine it;
And they have found out now I have no eyes
Of mortal lights, but certain influences,
Strange vertuous lightnings, humane nature starts at,
And I can kill my twenty in a morning,
With as much ease now—
Ha! what are these? new projects?
Where are my honourable Ladies? are you out too?
Nay then I must buy the stock, send me good Carding:
I hope the Princes hands be not in this sport;
I have not seen him yet, cannot hear from him,
And that troubles me: all these were recreations
Had I but his sweet company to laugh with me:
What fellow's that? another Apparition?
This is the lovingst Age: I should know that face,
Sure I have seen't before, not long since neither.

ANTIGONUS
She sees me now: O Heaven, a most rare creature!

CELIA
Yes, 'tis the same: I will take no notice of ye,
But if I do not fit ye, let me fry for't;
Is all this Cackling for your egg? they are fair ones,
Excellent rich no doubt too; and may stumble
A good staid mind, but I can go thus by 'em;
My honest friend; do you set off these Jewels?

ANTIGONUS
Set 'em off, Lady?

CELIA
I mean, sell 'em here, Sir?

ANTIGONUS
She's very quick; for sale they are not meant sure.

CELIA
For sanctity I think much less: good even Sir.

ANTIGONUS
Nay noble Lady, stay: 'tis you must wear 'em:
Never look strange, they are worthy your best beauty.

CELIA
Did you speak to me?

ANTIGONUS
To you or to none living:
To you they are sent, to you they are sacrificed.

CELIA
I'le never look a Horse i'th' mouth that's given:
I thank ye, Sir: I'le send one to reward ye.

ANTIGONUS
Do you never ask who sent 'em?

CELIA
Never I:
Nor never care, if it be an honest end,
That end's the full reward, and thanks but slubber it;
If it be ill, I will not urge the acquaintance.

ANTIGONUS
This has a soul indeed: pray let me tell ye—

CELIA
I care not if ye do, so you do it hansomly,
And not stand picking of your words.

ANTIGONUS
The King sent 'em.

CELIA
Away, away, thou art some foolish fellow,
And now I think thou hast stole 'em too: the King sent 'em?
Alas good man, wouldst thou make me believe
He has nothing to do with things of these worths,
But wantonly to fling 'em? he's an old man,
A good old man, they say too: I dare swear
Full many a year ago he left these gambols:
Here, take your trinkets.

ANTIGONUS
Sure I do not lye, Lady.

CELIA
I know thou lyest extreamly, damnably:
Thou hast a lying face.

ANTIGONUS

I was never thus ratled.

CELIA
But say I should believe: why are these sent me?
And why art thou the Messenger? who art thou?

ANTIGONUS
Lady, look on 'em wisely, and then consider
Who can send such as these, but a King only?
And, to what beauty can they be oblations,
But only yours? For me that am the carrier,
'Tis only fit you know I am his servant,
And have fulfil'd his will.

CELIA
You are short and pithy;
What must my beauty do for these?

ANTIGONUS
Sweet Lady,
You cannot be so hard of understanding,
When a King's favour shines upon ye gloriously,
And speaks his love in these—

CELIA
O then love's the matter;
Sir-reverence love; now I begin to feel ye:
And I should be the Kings Whore, a brave title;
And go as glorious as the Sun, O brave still:
The chief Commandress of his Concubines,
Hurried from place to place to meet his pleasures.

ANTIGONUS [aside]
A devilish subtil wench, but a rare spirit.

CELIA
And when the good old spunge had suckt my youth
And left some of his Royal aches in my bones:
When time shall tell me I have plough'd my life up,
And cast long furrows in my face to sink me.

ANTIGONUS
You must not think so, Lady.

CELIA
Then can these, Sir,
These precious things, the price of youth and beauty;
This shop here of sin-offerings set me off again?

Can it restore me chaste, young, innocent?
Purge me to what I was? add to my memory
An honest and a noble fame? The Kings device;
The sin's as universal as the Sun is,
And lights an everlasting Torch to shame me.

ANTIGONUS
Do you hold so sleight account of a great Kings favour,
That all knees bow to purchase?

CELIA
Prethee peace:
If thou knewst how ill favouredly thy tale becomes thee,
And what ill root it takes—

ANTIGONUS
You will be wiser.

CELIA
Could the King find no shape to shift his pander into,
But reverend Age? and one so like himself too?

ANTIGONUS
She has found me out.

CELIA
Cozen the world with gravity?
Prethee resolve me one thing, do's the King love thee?

ANTIGONUS
I think he do's.

CELIA
It seems so by thy Office:
He loves thy use, and when that's ended, hates thee:
Thou seemest to me a Souldier.

ANTIGONUS
Yes, I am one.

CELIA
And hast fought for thy Country?

ANTIGONUS
Many a time.

CELIA
May be, commanded too?

ANTIGONUS
I have done, Lady.

CELIA
O wretched man, below the state of pity!
Canst thou forget thou wert begot in honour?
A free Companion for a King? a Souldier?
Whose Nobleness dare feel no want, but Enemies?
Canst thou forget this, and decline so wretchedly,
To eat the Bread of Bawdry, of base Bawdry?
Feed on the scum of Sin? fling thy Sword from thee?
Dishonour to the noble name that nursed thee?
Go, beg diseases: let them be thy Armours,
Thy fights, the flames of Lust, and their foul issues.

ANTIGONUS
Why then I am a King, and mine own Speaker.

CELIA
And I as free as you, mine own Disposer:
There, take your Jewels; let them give them lustres
That have dark Lives and Souls; wear 'em your self, Sir,
You'l seem a Devil else.

ANTIGONUS
I command ye stay.

CELIA
Be just, I am commanded.

ANTIGONUS
I will not wrong ye.

CELIA
Then thus low falls my duty.

ANTIGONUS
Can ye love me?
Say I, and all I have—

CELIA
I cannot love ye;
Without the breach of faith I cannot hear ye;
Ye hang upon my love, like frosts on Lilies:
I can dye, but I cannot love: you are answer'd.

ANTIGONUS

I must find apter means, I love her truly.

SCÆNA SECUNDA

Enter **DEMETRIUS, LEONTIUS, LIEUTENANT, GENTLEMAN, SOULDIER** and **HOST**.

DEMETRIUS
Hither do you say she is come?

HOST
Yes Sir, I am sure on't:
For whilest I waited upon ye, putting my Wife in trust,
I know not by what means, but the King found her,
And hither she was brought; how, or to what end—

DEMETRIUS
My Father found her?

HOST
So my Wife informs me.

DEMETRIUS
Leontius, pray draw off the Souldiers,
I would a while be private.

LEONTIUS
Fall off Gentlemen,
The Prince would be alone.

[Exit **LEONTIUS** and **SOULDIER**.

DEMETRIUS
Is he so cunning?
There is some trick in this, and you must know it,
And be an agent too: which if it prove so—

HOST
Pull me to pieces, Sir.

DEMETRIUS
My Father found her?
My Father brought her hither? went she willingly?

HOST
My Wife sayes full of doubts.

DEMETRIUS
I cannot blame her,
No more: there's no trust, no faith in mankind.

[Enter **ANTIGONUS, MENIPPUS, LEONTIUS** and **SOULDIERS**.

ANTIGONUS
Keep her up close, he must not come to see her:
You are welcome nobly now, welcome home Gentlemen;
You have done a courteous service on the Enemy
Has tyed his Faith for ever; you shall find it;
Ye are not now in's debt Son: still your sad looks?
Leontius, what's the matter?

LEONTIUS
Truth Sir, I know not.
We have been merry since we went.

LIEUTENANT
I feel it.

ANTIGONUS
Come, what's the matter now? do you want mony?
Sure he has heard o'th' wench.

DEMETRIUS
Is that a want, Sir?
I would fain speak to your Grace.

ANTIGONUS
You may do freely.

DEMETRIUS
And not deserve your anger?

ANTIGONUS
That ye may too.

DEMETRIUS
There was a Gentlewoman, and sometimes my prisoner,
Which I thought well of Sir: your Grace conceives me.

ANTIGONUS
I do indeed, and with much grief conceive ye;
With full as much grief as your Mother bare you.
There was such a Woman: would I might as well say,
There was no such, Demetrius.

DEMETRIUS
She was vertuous,
And therefore not unfit my youth to love her:
She was as fair—

ANTIGONUS
Her beauty I'le proclaim too,
To be as rich as ever raign'd in Woman;
But how she made that good, the Devil knows.

DEMETRIUS
She was—O Heaven!

ANTIGONUS
The Hell to all thy glories,
Swallow'd thy youth, made shipwrack of thine honour:
She was a Devil.

DEMETRIUS
Ye are my father, Sir.

ANTIGONUS
And since ye take a pride to shew your follies,
I'le muster 'em, and all the world shall view 'em.

LEONTIUS
What heat is this? the Kings eyes speak his anger.

ANTIGONUS
Thou hast abus'd thy youth, drawn to thy fellowship
Instead of Arts and Arms, a Womans kisses,
The subtilties, and soft heats of a Harlot.

DEMETRIUS
Good Sir, mistake her not.

ANTIGONUS
A Witch, a Sorceress:
I tell thee but the truth; and hear Demetrius,
Which has so dealt upon thy bloud with charms,
Devilish and dark; so lockt up all thy vertues;
So pluckt thee back from what thou sprungst from, glorious.

DEMETRIUS
O Heaven, that any tongue but his durst say this!
That any heart durst harbour it! Dread Father,
If for the innocent the gods allow us
To bend our knees—

ANTIGONUS
Away, thou art bewitch'd still;
Though she be dead, her power still lives upon thee.

DEMETRIUS
Dead? O sacred Sir: dead did you say?

ANTIGONUS
She is dead, fool.

DEMETRIUS
It is not possible: be not so angry,
Say she is faln under your sad displeasure,
Or any thing but dead, say she is banished,
Invent a crime, and I'le believe it, Sir.

ANTIGONUS
Dead by the Law: we found her Hell, and her,
I mean her Charms and Spells, for which she perish'd;
And she confest she drew thee to thy ruine,
And purpos'd it, purpos'd my Empires overthrow.

DEMETRIUS
But is she dead? was there no pity Sir?
If her youth err'd, was there no mercy shown her?
Did ye look on her face, when ye condemn'd her?

ANTIGONUS
I look'd into her heart, and there she was hideous.

DEMETRIUS
Can she be dead? can vertue fall untimely?

ANTIGONUS
She is dead, deservingly she died.

DEMETRIUS
I have done then.
O matchless sweetness, whither art thou vanished?
O thou fair soul of all thy Sex, what Paradise
Hast thou inrich'd and blest? I am your son, Sir,
And to all you shall command stand most obedient,
Only a little time I must intreat you
To study to forget her; 'twill not be long, Sir,
Nor I long after it: art thou dead Celia,
Dead my poor wench? my joy, pluckt green with violence:
O fair sweet flower, farewel; Come, thou destroyer

Sorrow, thou melter of the soul, dwell with me;
Dwell with me solitary thoughts, tears, cryings,
Nothing that loves the day, love me, or seek me,
Nothing that loves his own life haunt about me:
And Love, I charge thee, never charm mine eyes more,
Nor ne're betray a beauty to my curses:
For I shall curse all now, hate all, forswear all,
And all the brood of fruitful nature vex at,
For she is gone that was all, and I nothing—

[Exit & **GENTLEMEN**.

ANTIGONUS
This opinion must be maintained.

MENIPPUS
It shall be, Sir.

ANTIGONUS
Let him go; I can at mine own pleasure
Draw him to th' right again: wait your instructions,
And see the souldier paid, Leontius:
Once more ye are welcome home all.

ALL
Health to your Majesty.

[Exit **ANTIGONUS** &c.

LEONTIUS
Thou wentest along the journey, how canst thou tell?

HOST
I did, but I am sure 'tis so: had I staid behind,
I think this had not proved.

LEONTIUS
A Wench the reason?

LIEUTENANT
Who's that talks of a Wench there?

LEONTIUS
All this discontent
About a Wench?

LIEUTENANT
Where is this Wench, good Colonel?

LEONTIUS
Prithee hold thy Peace: who calls thee to counsel?

LIEUTENANT
Why, if there be a Wench—

LEONTIUS
'Tis fit thou know her:

[Enter **TWO GENTLEMEN**.

That I'le say for thee, and as fit thou art for her,
Let her be mewed or stopt: how is it Gentlemen?

1ST GENTLEMAN
He's wondrous discontent, he'l speak to no man.

2ND GENTLEMAN
H'as taken his Chamber close, admits no entrance;
Tears in his eyes, and cryings out.

HOST
'Tis so, Sir,
And now I wish myself half hang'd ere I went this journey.

LEONTIUS
What is this Woman?

LIEUTENANT
I.

HOST
I cannot tell ye,
But handsome as Heaven.

LIEUTENANT
She is not so high I hope, Sir.

LEONTIUS
Where is she?

LIEUTENANT
I, that would be known.

LEONTIUS
Why, Sirrah.

HOST
I cannot show ye neither;
The King has now dispos'd of her.

LEONTIUS
There lyes the matter:
Will he admit none to come to comfort him?

1ST GENTLEMAN
Not any near, nor, let 'em knock their hearts out,
Will never speak.

LIEUTENANT
'Tis the best way if he have her;
For look you, a man would be loth to be disturb'd in's pastime;
'Tis every good mans case.

LEONTIUS
'Tis all thy living,
We must not suffer this, we dare not suffer it:
For when these tender souls meet deep afflictions,
They are not strong enough to struggle with 'em,
But drop away as Snow does, from a mountain,
And in the torrent of their own sighs sink themselves:
I will, and must speak to him.

LIEUTENANT
So must I too:
He promised me a charge.

LEONTIUS
Of what? of Children
Upon my Conscience, thou hast a double company,
And all of thine own begetting already.

LIEUTENANT
That's all one,
I'le raise 'em to a Regiment, and then command 'em,
When they turn disobedient, unbeget 'em:
Knock 'em o'th' head, and put in new.

LEONTIUS
A rare way;
But for all this, thou art not valiant enough
To dare to see the Prince now?

LIEUTENANT
Do ye think he's angry?

1ST GENTLEMAN
Extreamly vext.

2ND GENTLEMAN
To the endangering of any man comes near him.

1ST GENTLEMAN
Yet, if thou couldst but win him out,
What e're thy suit were,
Believe it granted presently.

LEONTIUS
Yet thou must think though,
That in the doing he may break upon ye,
And—

LIEUTENANT
If he do not kill me.

LEONTIUS
There's the question.

LIEUTENANT
For half a dozen hurts.

LEONTIUS
Art thou so valiant?

LIEUTENANT
Not absolutely so neither: no it cannot be,
I want my impostumes, and my things about me,
Yet I'le make danger, Colonel.

LEONTIUS
'Twill be rare sport,
Howe're it take; give me thy hand; if thou dost this,
I'le raise thee up a horse Troop, take my word for't.

LIEUTENANT
What may be done by humane man.

LEONTIUS
Let's go then.

1ST GENTLEMAN
Away before he cool: he will relapse else.

[Exit.

SCÆNA TERTIA

Enter **ANTIGONUS**, **MENIPPUS** and **LEUCIPPE**.

ANTIGONUS
Will she not yield?

LEUCIPPE
For all we can urge to her;
I swore you would marry her, she laugh'd extreamly,
And then she rail'd like thunder.

ANTIGONUS
Call in the Magician.

[Enter **MAGICIAN** with a Bowl.

I must, and will obtain her, I am ashes else.
Are all the Philters in? Charms, Powders, Roots?

MAGICIAN
They are all in; and now I only stay
The invocation of some helping Spirits.

ANTIGONUS
To your work then, and dispatch.

MAGICIAN
Sit still, and fear not.

LEUCIPPE
I shall ne'r endure these sights.

ANTIGONUS
Away with the Woman: go wait without.

[Exit.

LEUCIPPE
When the Devil's gone, pray call me.

ANTIGONUS
Be sure you make it powerful enough.

MAGICIAN
Pray doubt not—

[He Conjures.

A SONG.

Rise from the Shades below,
All you that prove
The helps of looser Love;
Rise and bestow
Upon this Cup, what ever may compel
By powerful Charm, and unresisted Spell,
A Heart un-warm'd to melt in Loves desires.
Distill into this Liquor all your fires:
Heats, longings, tears,
But keep back frozen fears;
That she may know, that has all power defied,
Art is a power that will not be denied.

The ANSWER.

I Obey, I Obey,
And am come to view the day,
Brought along, all may compel,
All the Earth has, and our Hell:
Here's a little, little Flower,
This will make her sweat an hour,
Then unto such flames arise,
A thousand joys will not suffice.
Here's the powder of the Moon,
With which she caught Endymion;
The powerful tears that Venus cryed,
When the Boy Adonis dyed,
Here's Medea's Charm, with which
Jasons heart she did bewitch,
Omphale this Spell put in,
When she made the Libyan spin.
This dull root pluckt from Lethe flood,
Purges all pure thoughts, and good.
These I stir thus, round, round, round,
Whilst our light feet beat the ground.

MAGICIAN
Now Sir, 'tis full, and whosoever drinks this
Shall violently doat upon your person,
And never sleep nor eat unsatisfied:

So many hours 'twill work, and work with Violence;
And those expired, 'tis done. You have my art, Sir.

[Enter **LEUCIPPE**.

ANTIGONUS
See him rewarded liberally—Leucippe.
Here, take this bowl, and when she calls for Wine next,
Be sure you give her this, and see her drink it;
Delay no time when she calls next.

LEUCIPPE
I shall, Sir.

ANTIGONUS
Let none else touch it on your life.

LEUCIPPE
I am charg'd, Sir.

ANTIGONUS
Now if she have an antidote art let her 'scape me.

[Exeunt.

SCÆNA QUARTA

Enter **LEONTIUS, LIEUTENANT, GENTLEMAN**.

1ST GENTLEMAN
There's the door, Lieutenant, if you dare do any thing.

LEONTIUS
Here's no man waits.

1ST GENTLEMAN
H' as given a charge that none shall,
Nor none shall come within the hearing of him:
Dare ye go forward?

LIEUTENANT
Let me put on my Skull first.
My head's almost beaten into th' pap of an Apple.
Are there no Guns i'th' door?

LEONTIUS

The Rogue will do it.
And yet I know he has no Stomach to't.

LIEUTENANT
What loop-holes are there when I knock for stones,
For those may pepper me? I can perceive none.

LEONTIUS
How he views the Fortification.

LIEUTENANT
Farewel Gentlemen,
If I be kill'd—

LEONTIUS
We'll see thee buried bravely.

LIEUTENANT
Away, how should I know that then? I'll knock softly.
Pray heaven he speak in a low voice now to comfort me:
I feel I have no heart to't:—Is't well, Gentlemen?
Colonel, my Troop—

LEONTIUS
A little louder.

LIEUTENANT
Stay, stay;
Here is a window, I will see, stand wide.
By Heav'n—he's charging of a Gun.

LEONTIUS
There's no such matter.
There's no body in this room.

LIEUTENANT
O 'twas a fire-shovel:
Now I'll knock louder; if he say who's there?
As sure he has so much manners, then will I answer him
So finely & demurely; my Troop Colonel—

[Knocks louder.

1ST GENTLEMAN
Knock louder, Fool, he hears not.

LIEUTENANT
You fool, do you.

Do and you dare now.

1ST GENTLEMAN
I do not undertake it.

LIEUTENANT
Then hold your peace, and meddle with your own matters.

LEONTIUS
Now he will knock.

[Knocks louder.

LIEUTENANT
Sir, Sir, will't please you hear Sir?
Your Grace, I'll look again, what's that?

LEONTIUS
He's there now.
Lord! How he stares! I ne'r yet saw him thus alter'd:
Stand now, and take the Troop.

LIEUTENANT
Would I were in't,
And a good horse under me: I must knock again,
The Devil's at my fingers ends: he comes now.
Now Colonel, if I live—

LEONTIUS
The Troop's thine own Boy.

[Enter **DEMETRIUS**, a Pistol.

DEMETRIUS
What desperate fool, ambitious of his ruine?

LIEUTENANT
Your Father would desire ye, Sir, to come to dinner.

DEMETRIUS
Thou art no more.

LIEUTENANT
Now, now, now, now.

DEMETRIUS
Poor Coxcomb:
Why do I aim at thee?

[Exit.

LEONTIUS
His fear has kill'd him.

[Enter **LEUCIPPE** with a Bowl.

2ND GENTLEMAN
I protest he's almost stiff: bend him and rub him,
Hold his Nose close, you, if you be a woman,
Help us a little: here's a man near perish'd.

LEUCIPPE
Alas alas, I have nothing here about me.
Look to my Bowl; I'll run in presently
And fetch some water: bend him, and set him upwards.

LEONTIUS
A goodly man—

[Exit.

Here's a brave heart: he's warm again: you shall not
Leave us i'th' lurch so, Sirrah.

2ND GENTLEMAN
Now he breaths too.

LEONTIUS
If we had but any drink to raise his Spirits.
What's that i'th' Bowl? upon my life, good Liquor,
She would not own it else.

1ST GENTLEMAN
He sees.

LEONTIUS
Look up Boy.
And take this Cup, and drink it off; I'll pledge thee.
Guide it to his mouth, he swallows heartily.

2ND GENTLEMAN
Oh! fear and sorrow's dry; 'tis off—

LEONTIUS
Stand up man.

LIEUTENANT
Am I not shot?

LEONTIUS
Away with him, and chear him:
Thou hast won thy Troop.

LIEUTENANT
I think I won it bravely.

LEONTIUS
Go, I must see the Prince, he must not live thus;
And let me hear an hour hence from ye.
Well, Sir—

[Exeunt **GENTLEMAN** and **LIEUTENANT**.

[Enter **LEUCIPPE** with water.

LEUCIPPE
Here, here: where's the sick Gentleman?

LEONTIUS
He's up, and gone, Lady.

LEUCIPPE
Alas, that I came so late.

LEONTIUS
He must still thank ye;
Ye left that in a Cup here did him comfort.

LEUCIPPE
That in the Bowl?

LEONTIUS
Yes truly, very much comfort,
He drank it off, and after it spoke lustily.

LEUCIPPE
Did he drink it all?

LEONTIUS
All off.

LEUCIPPE
The Devil choak him;
I am undone: h'as twenty Devils in him;

Undone for ever, left he none?

LEONTIUS
I think not.

LEUCIPPE
No, not a drop: what shall become of me now?
Had he no where else to swound? a vengeance swound him:
Undone, undone, undone: stay, I can lye yet
And swear too at a pinch, that's all my comfort.
Look to him; I say look to him, & but mark what follows.

[Exit.

[Enter **DEMETRIUS**.

LEONTIUS
What a Devil ails the Woman? here comes the Prince again,
With such a sadness on his face, as sorrow,
Sorrow her self but poorly imitates.
Sorrow of Sorrows on that heart that caus'd it.

DEMETRIUS
Why might she not be false and treacherous to me?
And found so by my Father? she was a Woman,
And many a one of that Sex, young and fair,
As full of faith as she, have fallen, and foully.

LEONTIUS
It is a Wench! O that I knew the circumstance.

DEMETRIUS
Why might not, to preserve me from this ruine,
She having lost her honour, and abused me,
My father change the forms o'th' coins, and execute
His anger on a fault she ne'r committed,
Only to keep me safe? why should I think so?
She never was to me, but all obedience,
Sweetness, and love.

LEONTIUS
How heartily he weeps now!
I have not wept this thirty years, and upward;
But now, if I should be hang'd I cannot hold from't
It grieves me to the heart.

DEMETRIUS
Who's that that mocks me?

LEONTIUS
A plague of him that mocks ye: I grieve truly,
Truly, and heartily to see you thus, Sir:
And if it lay in my power, gods are my witness,
Who e'r he be that took your sweet peace from you;
I am not so old yet, nor want I spirit—

DEMETRIUS
No more of that, no more Leontius,
Revenges are the gods: our part is sufferance:
Farewell, I shall not see thee long.

LEONTIUS
Good Sir, tell me the cause, I know there is a woman in't;
Do you hold me faithful? dare you trust your Souldier?
Sweet Prince, the cause?

DEMETRIUS
I must not, dare not tell it,
And as thou art an honest man, enquire not.

LEONTIUS
Will ye be merry then?

DEMETRIUS
I am wondrous merry.

LEONTIUS
'Tis wondrous well: you think now this becomes ye.
Shame on't, it does not, Sir, it shews not handsomely;
If I were thus; you would swear I were an Ass straight;
A wooden ass; whine for a Wench?

DEMETRIUS
Prithee leave me.

LEONTIUS
I will not leave ye for a tit.

DEMETRIUS
Leontius?

LEONTIUS
For that you may have any where for six pence,
And a dear penny-worth too.

DEMETRIUS

Nay, then you are troublesome.

LEONTIUS
Not half so troublesom as you are to your self, Sir;
Was that brave Heart made to pant for a placket:
And now i'th' dog-days too, when nothing dare love!
That noble Mind to melt away and moulder
For a hey nonny, nonny! Would I had a Glass here,
To shew ye what a pretty toy ye are turn'd to.

DEMETRIUS
My wretched Fortune.

LEONTIUS
Will ye but let me know her?
I'll once turn Bawd: go to, they are good mens offices,
And not so contemptible as we take 'em for:
And if she be above ground, and a Woman;
I ask no more; I'll bring her o' my back, Sir,
By this hand I will, and I had as lieve bring the Devil,
I care not who she be, nor where I have her;
And in your arms, or the next Bed deliver her,
Which you think fittest, and when you have danc'd your galliard.

DEMETRIUS
Away, and fool to them are so affected:
O thou art gone, and all my comfort with thee!
Wilt thou do one thing for me?

LEONTIUS
All things i'th' World, Sir,
Of all dangers.

DEMETRIUS
Swear.

LEONTIUS
I will.

DEMETRIUS
Come near me no more then.

LEONTIUS
How?

DEMETRIUS
Come no more near me:
Thou art a plague-sore to me.

[Exit.

LEONTIUS
Give you good ev'n Sir;
If you be suffer'd thus, we shall have fine sport.
I will be sorry yet.

[Enter **TWO GENTLEMEN**.

1ST GENTLEMAN
How now, how does he?

LEONTIUS
Nay, if I tell ye, hang me, or any man else
That hath his nineteen wits; he has the bots I think,
He groans, and roars, and kicks.

2ND GENTLEMAN
Will he speak yet?

LEONTIUS
Not willingly:
Shortly he will not see a man; if ever
I look'd upon a Prince so metamorphos'd,
So juggl'd into I know not what, shame take me;
This 'tis to be in love.

1ST GENTLEMAN
Is that the cause on't?

LEONTIUS
What is it not the cause of but bear-baitings?
And yet it stinks much like it: out upon't;
What giants, and what dwarffs, what owls and apes,
What dogs, and cats it makes us? men that are possest with it,
Live as if they had a Legion of Devils in 'em,
And every Devil of a several nature;
Nothing but Hey-pass, re-pass: where's the Lieutenant?
Has he gather'd up the end on's wits again?

1ST GENTLEMAN
He is alive: but you that talk of wonders,
Shew me but such a wonder as he is now.

LEONTIUS
Why? he was ever at the worst a wonder.

2ᴺᴰ GENTLEMAN
He is now most wonderful; a Blazer now, Sir.

LEONTIUS
What ails the Fool? and what Star reigns now Gentlemen
We have such Prodigies?

2ᴺᴰ GENTLEMAN
'Twill pose your heaven-hunters;
He talks now of the King, no other language,
And with the King as he imagines, hourly.
Courts the King, drinks to the King, dies for the King,
Buys all the Pictures of the King, wears the Kings colours.

LEONTIUS
Does he not lye i'th' King street too?

1ˢᵀ GENTLEMAN
He's going thither,
Makes prayers for the King, in sundry languages,
Turns all his Proclamations into metre;
Is really in love with the King, most dotingly,
And swears Adonis was a Devil to him:
A sweet King, a most comely King, and such a King—

2ᴺᴰ GENTLEMAN
Then down on's marrow-bones; O excellent King
Thus he begins, Thou Light, and Life of Creatures,
Angel-ey'd King, vouchsafe at length thy favour;
And so proceeds to incision: what think ye of this sorrow?

1ˢᵀ GENTLEMAN
Will as familiarly kiss the King's horses
As they pass by him: ready to ravish his footman.

LEONTIUS
Why, this is above Ela?
But how comes this?

1ˢᵀ GENTLEMAN
Nay that's to understand yet,
But thus it is, and this part but the poorest,
'Twould make a man leap over the Moon to see him act these.

2ᴺᴰ GENTLEMAN
With sighs as though his heart would break:
Cry like a breech'd boy, not eat a bit.

LEONTIUS
I must go see him presently,
For this is such a gig, for certain, Gentlemen,
The Fiend rides on a Fiddle-stick.

2ND GENTLEMAN
I think so.

LEONTIUS
Can ye guide me to him for half an hour? I am his
To see the miracle.

1ST GENTLEMAN
We sure shall start him.

[Exeunt.

SCÆNA QUINTA

Enter **ANTIGONUS** and **LEUCIPPE**.

ANTIGONUS
Are you sure she drank it?

LEUCIPPE
Now must I lye most confidently.
Yes Sir, she has drunk it off.

ANTIGONUS
How works it with her?

LEUCIPPE
I see no alteration yet.

ANTIGONUS
There will be,
For he is the greatest Artist living made it.
Where is she now?

LEUCIPPE
She is ready to walk out, Sir.

ANTIGONUS
Stark mad, I know she will be.

LEUCIPPE

So I hope, Sir.

ANTIGONUS
She knows not of the Prince?

LEUCIPPE
Of no man living—

ANTIGONUS
How do I look? how do my cloaths become me?
I am not very grey.

LEUCIPPE
A very youth, Sir,
Upon my maiden-head as smug as April:
Heaven bless that sweet face, 'twill undo a thousand;
Many a soft heart must sob yet, e'r that wither,
Your Grace can give content enough.

[Enter **CELIA** with a Book.

ANTIGONUS
I think so.

LEUCIPPE
Here she comes, Sir.

ANTIGONUS
How shall I keep her off me?
Go, & perfume the room: make all things ready.

[Exit **LEUCIPPE**.

CELIA
No hope yet of the Prince! no comfort of him!
They keep me mew'd up here, as they mew mad folks,
No company but my afflictions.
This royal Devil again! strange, how he haunts me!
How like a poyson'd potion his eyes fright me!
Has made himself handsome too.

ANTIGONUS
Do you look now, Lady?
You will leap anon.

CELIA
Curl'd and perfum'd? I smell him;
He looks on's legs too, sure he will cut a caper;

God-a-mercy, dear December.

ANTIGONUS
O do you smile now;
I knew it would work with you; come hither pretty one.

CELIA
Sir.

ANTIGONUS
I like those courtesies well; come hither and kiss me.

CELIA
I am reading, Sir, of a short Treatise here,
That's call'd the Vanity of Lust: has your Grace seen it?
He says here, that an Old Mans loose desire
Is like the Glow-worms light, the Apes so wonder'd at:
Which when they gather'd sticks, and laid upon't,
And blew, and blew, turn'd tail, and went out presently:
And in another place he calls their loves,
Faint Smells of dying Flowers, carry no comforts;
They're doting, stinking foggs, so thick and muddy,
Reason with all his beams cannot beat through 'em.

ANTIGONUS
How's this? is this the potion? you but fool still;
I know you love me.

CELIA
As you are just and honest;
I know I love and honour you: admire you.

ANTIGONUS
This makes against me, fearfully against me.

CELIA
But as you bring your power to persecute me,
Your traps to catch mine innocence to rob me,
As you lay out your lusts to overwhelm me,
Hell never hated good, as I hate you, Sir;
And I dare tell it to your face: What glory
Now after all your Conquests got, your Titles,
The ever-living memories rais'd to you,
Can my defeat be? my poor wrack, what triumph?
And when you crown your swelling Cups to fortune,
What honourable tongue can sing my story?
Be as your Emblem is, a glorious Lamp
Set on the top of all, to light all perfectly:

Be as your office is, a god-like Justice,
Into all shedding equally your Vertues.

ANTIGONUS
She has drencht me now; now I admire her goodness;
So young, so nobly strong, I never tasted:
Can nothing in the power of Kings perswade ye?

CELIA
No, nor that power command me.

ANTIGONUS
Say I should force ye?
I have it in my will.

CELIA
Your will's a poor one;
And though it be a King's Will, a despised one.
Weaker than Infants legs, your will's in swadling Clouts,
A thousand ways my will has found to check ye;
A thousand doors to 'scape ye, I dare dye, Sir;
As suddenly I dare dye, as you can offer:
Nay, say you had your Will, say you had ravish'd me,
Perform'd your lust, what had you purchas'd by it?
What Honour won? do you know who dwells above, Sir,
And what they have prepar'd for men turn'd Devils?
Did you never hear their thunder? start and tremble,
Death sitting on your bloud, when their fires visit us.
Will nothing wring you then do you think? sit hard here,
And like a Snail curl round about your Conscience,
Biting and stinging: will you not roar too late then?
Then when you shake in horrour of this Villainy,
Then will I rise a Star in Heaven, and scorn ye.

ANTIGONUS
Lust, how I hate thee now! and love this sweetness!
Will you be my Queen? can that price purchase ye?

CELIA
Not all the World, I am a Queen already,
Crown'd by his Love, I must not lose for Fortune;
I can give none away, sell none away, Sir,
Can lend no love, am not mine own Exchequer;
For in anothers heart my hope and peace lies.

ANTIGONUS
Your fair hands, Lady? for yet I am not pure enough
To touch these Lips, in that sweet Peace ye spoke of.

Live now for ever, and I to serve your Vertues—

CELIA
Why now you show a god! now I kneel to ye;
This Sacrifice of Virgins Joy send to ye:
Thus I hold up my hands to Heaven that touch'd ye,
And pray eternal Blessings dwell about ye.

ANTIGONUS
Vertue commands the Stars: rise more than Vertue;
Your present comfort shall be now my business.

CELIA
All my obedient service wait upon ye.

[Exit severally.

SCÆNA SEXTA

Enter **LEONTIUS**, **GENTLEMEN** and **LIEUTENANT**.

LEONTIUS
Hast thou clean forgot the Wars?

LIEUTENANT
Prithee hold thy peace.

1ST GENTLEMAN
His mind's much elevated now.

LEONTIUS
It seems so.
Sirrah.

LIEUTENANT
I am so troubled with this Fellow.

LEONTIUS
He will call me Rogue anon.

1ST GENTLEMAN
'Tis ten to one else.

LIEUTENANT
O King that thou knew'st I lov'd thee, how I lov'd thee.
And where O King, I barrel up thy beauty.

LEONTIUS
He cannot leave his Sutlers trade, he woos in't.

LIEUTENANT
O never, King.

LEONTIUS
By this hand, when I consider—

LIEUTENANT
My honest friend, you are a little sawcy.

1ST GENTLEMAN
I told you you would have it.

LIEUTENANT
When mine own worth—

LEONTIUS
Is flung into the ballance, and found nothing.

LIEUTENANT
And yet a Soldier.

LEONTIUS
And yet a sawcy one.

LIEUTENANT
One that has followed thee.

LEONTIUS
Fair and far off.

LIEUTENANT
Fought for thy grace.

LEONTIUS
'Twas for some grief, you lye Sir.

LIEUTENANT
He's the son of a whore denies this: will that satisfie ye?

LEONTIUS
Yes, very well.

LIEUTENANT
Shall then that thing that honours thee?

How miserable a thing soever, yet a thing still;
And though a thing of nothing, thy thing ever.

LEONTIUS
Here's a new thing.

2ND GENTLEMAN
He's in a deep dump now.

LEONTIUS
I'le fetch him out on't. When's the King's birth-day?

LIEUTENANT
When e're it be, that day I'le dye with ringing.
And there's the resolution of a Lover.

[Exit.

LEONTIUS
A goodly resolution sure I take it.
He is bewitch'd, or moop'd, or his brains melted,
Could he find no body to fall in love with; but the King,
The good old King, to doat upon him too?
Stay, now I remember, what the fat woman warn'd me,
Bid me remember, and look to him too:
I'le hang if she have not a hand in this: he's conjured,
Goe after him, I pity the poor Rascal,
In the mean time I'le wait occasion
To work upon the Prince.

2ND GENTLEMAN
Pray doe that seriously.

[Exit severally.

SCAENA SEPTIMA

Enter **ANTIGONUS, MENIPPUS, LORDS**.

LORD
He's very ill.

ANTIGONUS
I am very sorry for't,
And much ashamed I have wronged her innocence,
Menippus, guide her to the Princes lodgings,

There leave her to his love again.

MENIPPUS
I am glad Sir.

LORD
He will speak to none.

ANTIGONUS
O I shall break that silence;
Be quick, take fair attendance.

MENIPPUS
Yes Sir presently.

[Exit.

ANTIGONUS
He will find his tongue, I warrant ye; his health too;
I send a physick will not fail.

LORD
Fair work it.

ANTIGONUS
We hear the Princes mean to visit us
In way of truce.

LORD
'Tis thought so.

ANTIGONUS
Come: let's in then,
And think upon the noblest wayes to meet 'em.

[Exeunt.

SCÆNA OCTAVIA

Enter **LEONTIUS**.

LEONTIUS
There's no way now to get in: all the light stopt too;
Nor can I hear a sound of him, pray Heaven
He use no violence: I think he has more Soul,
Stronger, and I hope nobler: would I could but see once,

This beauty he groans under, or come to know
But any circumstance. What noise is that there?
I think I heard him groan: here are some coming;
A woman too, I'le stand aloof, and view 'em.

[Enter **MENIPPUS, CELIA, LORDS**.

CELIA
Well, some of ye have been to blame in this point,
But I forgive ye: The King might have pickt out too
Some fitter woman to have tri'd his valour.

MENIPPUS
'Twas all to the best meant, Lady.

CELIA
I must think so,
For how to mend it now: he's here you tell me?

MENIPPUS
He's Madam, and the joy to see you only
Will draw him out.

LEONTIUS
I know that womans tongue,
I think I have seen her face too: I'le goe nearer:
If this be she, he has some cause of sorrow:
'Tis the same face; the same, most excellent woman.

CELIA
This should be Lord Leontius: I remember him.

LEONTIUS
Lady, I think ye know me.

CELIA
Speak soft, good Souldier:
I do, and know ye worthy, know ye noble;
Know not me yet openly, as you love me;
But let me see ye again, I'le satisfie ye:
I am wondrous glad to see those eyes.

LEONTIUS
You have charged me.

CELIA
You shall know where I am.

LEONTIUS
I will not off yet:
She goes to knock at's door: This must be she
The fellow told me of: right glad I am on't,
He will bolt now for certain.

CELIA
Are ye within Sir?
I'le trouble you no more: I thank your courtesie,
Pray leave me now.

ALL
Me. We rest your humble servants.

[Exit **MENIPPUS** &c.

CELIA
So now my jives are off: pray Heaven he be here!
Master, my royal Sir: do you hear who calls ye?
Love, my Demetrius.

LEONTIUS
These are pretty quail-pipes,
The Cock will Crow anon.

CELIA
Can ye be drowsie,
When I call at your Window?

LEONTIUS
I hear him stirring:
Now he comes wondring out.

[Enter **DEMETRIUS**.

DEMETRIUS
'Tis Celias sound sure:
The sweetness of that tongue draws all hearts to it;
There stands the shape too.

LEONTIUS
How he stares upon her!

DEMETRIUS
Ha? do mine eyes abuse me?
'Tis she, the living Celia: your hand Lady?

CELIA

What should this mean?

DEMETRIUS
The very self same Celia.

CELIA
How do ye Sir?

DEMETRIUS
Only turn'd brave.
I heard you were dead my dear one, compleat,
She is wondrous brave, a wondrous gallant Courtier.

CELIA
How he surveyes me round? here has been foul play.

DEMETRIUS
How came she thus?

CELIA
It was a kind of death Sir,
I suffered in your absence, mew'd up here,
And kept conceal'd I know not how.

DEMETRIUS
'Tis likely:
How came you hither Celia? wondrous gallant:
Did my Father send for ye?

CELIA
So they told me Sir,
And on command too.

DEMETRIUS
I hope you were obedient?

CELIA
I was so ever.

DEMETRIUS
And ye were bravely us'd?

CELIA
I wanted nothing:
My maiden-head to a mote i'th' Sun, he's jealous:
I must now play the knave with him, though I dye for't,
'Tis in my nature.

DEMETRIUS
Her very eyes are alter'd:
Jewels, and rich ones too, I never saw yet—
And what were those came for ye?

CELIA
Monstrous jealous:
Have I liv'd at the rate of these scorn'd questions?
They seem'd of good sort, Gentlemen.

DEMETRIUS
Kind men?

CELIA
They were wondrous kind:
I was much beholding to 'em;
There was one Menippus Sir.

DEMETRIUS
Ha?

CELIA
One Menippus,
A notable merry Lord, and a good companion.

DEMETRIUS
And one Charinthus too?

CELIA
Yes, there was such a one.

DEMETRIUS
And Timon?

CELIA
'Tis most true.

DEMETRIUS
And thou most treacherous:
My Fathers bawds by—they never miss course;
And were these daily with ye?

CELIA
Every hour Sir.

DEMETRIUS
And was there not a Lady, a fat Lady?

CELIA
O yes; a notable good wench.

DEMETRIUS
The Devil fetch her.

CELIA
'Tis ev'n the merriest wench—

DEMETRIUS
Did she keep with ye too?

CELIA
She was all in all; my bed-fellow, eat with me,
Brought me acquainted.

DEMETRIUS
You are well known here then?

CELIA
There is no living here a stranger I think.

DEMETRIUS
How came ye by this brave gown?

CELIA
This is a poor one:
Alas, I have twenty richer: do you see these jewels?
Why, they are the poorest things, to those are sent me,
And sent me hourly too.

DEMETRIUS
Is there no modestie?
No faith in this fair Sex?

LEONTIUS
What will this prove too?
For yet with all my wits, I understand not.

DEMETRIUS
Come hither; thou art dead indeed, lost, tainted;
All that I left thee fair, and innocent,
Sweet as thy youth, and carrying comfort in't;
All that I hoped for vertuous, is fled from thee,
Turn'd black, and bankrupt.

LEONTIUS
'By'r Lady, this cuts shrewdly.

DEMETRIUS
Thou art dead, for ever dead; sins surfeit slew thee;
The ambition of those wanton eyes betrai'd thee;
Go from me, grave of honour; go thou foul one,
Thou glory of thy sin; go thou despis'd one,
And where there is no vertue, nor no virgin;
Where Chastity was never known, nor heard of;
Where nothing reigns but impious lust, and looser faces.
Go thither, child of bloud, and sing my doating.

CELIA
You do not speak this seriously I hope Sir;
I did but jest with you.

DEMETRIUS
Look not upon me,
There is more hell in those eyes, than hell harbours;
And when they flame, more torments.

CELIA
Dare ye trust me?
You durst once even with all you had: your love Sir?
By this fair light I am honest.

DEMETRIUS
Thou subtle Circe,
Cast not upon the maiden light eclipses:
Curse not the day.

CELIA
Come, come, you shall not do this:
How fain you would seem angry now, to fright me;
You are not in the field among your Enemies;
Come, I must cool this courage.

DEMETRIUS
Out thou impudence,
Thou ulcer of thy Sex; when I first saw thee,
I drew into mine eyes mine own destruction,
I pull'd into my heart that sudden poyson,
That now consumes my dear content to cinders:
I am not now Demetrius, thou hast chang'd me;
Thou, woman, with thy thousand wiles hast chang'd me;
Thou Serpent with thy angel-eyes hast slain me;
And where, before I touch'd on this fair ruine,
I was a man, and reason made, and mov'd me,
Now one great lump of grief, I grow and wander.

CELIA
And as you are noble, do you think I did this?

DEMETRIUS
Put all the Devils wings on, and flie from me.

CELIA
I will go from ye, never more to see ye:
I will flie from ye, as a plague hangs o're me;
And through the progress of my life hereafter;
Where ever I shall find a fool, a false man,
One that ne're knew the worth of polish'd vertue;
A base suspecter of a virgins honour,
A child that flings away the wealth he cri'd for,
Him will I call Demetrius: that fool Demetrius,
That mad man a Demetrius; and that false man,
The Prince of broken faiths, even Prince Demetrius.
You think now, I should cry, and kneel down to ye,
Petition for my peace; let those that feel here
The weight of evil, wait for such a favour,
I am above your hate, as far above it,
In all the actions of an innocent life,
As the pure Stars are from the muddy meteors,
Cry when you know your folly: howl and curse then,
Beat that unmanly breast, that holds a false heart
When ye shall come to know, whom ye have flung from ye.

DEMETRIUS
Pray ye stay a little.

CELIA
Not your hopes can alter me.
Then let a thousand black thoughts muster in ye,
And with those enter in a thousand doatings;
Those eyes be never shut, but drop to nothing:
My innocence for ever haunt and fright ye:
Those arms together grow in folds; that tongue,
That bold bad tongue that barks out these disgraces.
When you shall come to know how nobly vertuous
I have preserv'd my life, rot, rot within ye.

DEMETRIUS
What shall I doe?

CELIA
Live a lost man for ever.
Go ask your Fathers conscience what I suffered,

And through what seas of hazards I sayl'd through:
Mine honour still advanced in spight of tempests,
Then take your leave of love; and confess freely,
You were never worthy of this heart that serv'd ye,
And so farewel ungratefull—

[Exit.

DEMETRIUS
Is she gone?

LEONTIUS
I'le follow her, and will find out this matter.—

[Exit.

[Enter **ANTIGONUS** and **LORDS**.

ANTIGONUS
Are ye pleas'd now? have you got your heart again?
Have I restor'd ye that?

DEMETRIUS
Sir even for Heaven sake,
And sacred truth sake, tell me how ye found her.

ANTIGONUS
I will, and in few words. Before I tri'd her,
'Tis true, I thought her most unfit your fellowship,
And fear'd her too: which fear begot that story
I told ye first: but since, like gold I toucht her.

DEMETRIUS
And how dear Sir?

ANTIGONUS
Heavens holy light's not purer:
The constancy and goodness of all women
That ever liv'd, to win the names of worthy,
This noble Maid has doubled in her: honour,
All promises of wealth, all art to win her,
And by all tongues imploy'd, wrought as much on her
As one may doe upon the Sun at noon day
By lighting Candles up: her shape is heavenly,
And to that heavenly shape her thoughts are angels.

DEMETRIUS
Why did you tell me Sir?

ANTIGONUS
'Tis true, I err'd in't:
But since I made a full proof of her vertue,
I find a King too poor a servant for her.
Love her, and honour her; in all observe her.
She must be something more than time yet tells her:
And certain I believe him blest, enjoyes her:
I would not lose the hope of such a Daughter,
To adde another Empire to my honour.—

[Exit.

DEMETRIUS
O wretched state! to what end shall I turn me?
And where begins my penance? now, what service
Will win her love again? my death must doe it:
And if that sacrifice can purge my follies,
Be pleas'd, O mightie Love, I dye thy servant—

[Exit.

ACTUS QUINTUS

SCÆNA PRIMA

Enter **LEONTIUS** and **CELIA**.

LEONTIUS
I know he do's not deserve ye; h'as us'd you poorly:
And to redeem himself—

CELIA
Redeem?

LEONTIUS
I know it—
There's no way left.

CELIA
For Heavens sake do not name him,
Do not think on him Sir, he's so far from me
In all my thoughts now, methinks I never knew him.

LEONTIUS
But yet I would see him again.

CELIA
No, never, never.

LEONTIUS
I do not mean to lend him any comfort;
But to afflict him, so to torture him;
That even his very Soul may shake within him:
To make him know, though he be great and powerfull,
'Tis not within his aim to deal dishonourably,
And carry it off; and with a maid of your sort.

CELIA
I must confess, I could most spightfully afflict him;
Now, now, I could whet my anger at him;
Now arm'd with bitterness, I could shoot through him;
I long to vex him.

LEONTIUS
And doe it home, and bravely.

CELIA
Were I a man!

LEONTIUS
I'le help that weakness in ye:
I honour ye, and serve ye.

CELIA
Not only to disclaim me,
When he had seal'd his vowes in Heaven, sworn to me,
And poor believing I became his servant:
But most maliciously to brand my credit,
Stain my pure name.

LEONTIUS
I would not suffer it:
See him I would again, and to his teeth too:
Od's precious, I would ring him such a lesson—

CELIA
I have done that already.

LEONTIUS
Nothing, nothing:
It was too poor a purge; besides, by this time
He has found his fault, and feels the hells that follow it.
That, and your urg'd on anger to the highest,

Why, 'twill be such a stroak—

CELIA
Say he repent then,
And seek with tears to soften, I am a woman;
A woman that have lov'd him, Sir, have honour'd him:
I am no more.

LEONTIUS
Why, you may deal thereafter.

CELIA
If I forgive him, I am lost.

LEONTIUS
Hold there then,
The sport will be to what a poor submission—
But keep you strong.

CELIA
I would not see him.

LEONTIUS
Yes,
You shall Ring his knell.

CELIA
How if I kill him?

LEONTIUS
Kill him? why, let him dye.

CELIA
I know 'tis fit so.
But why should I that lov'd him once, destroy him?
O had he scap't this sin, what a brave Gentleman—

LEONTIUS
I must confess, had this not faln, a nobler,
A handsomer, the whole world had not show'd ye:
And to his making such a mind—

CELIA
'Tis certain:
But all this I must now forget.

LEONTIUS
You shall not

If I have any art: goe up sweet Lady,
And trust my truth.

CELIA
But good Sir bring him not.

LEONTIUS
I would not for the honour ye are born to,
But you shall see him, and neglect him too, and scorn him.

CELIA
You will be near me then.

LEONTIUS
I will be with ye;
Yet there's some hope to stop this gap, I'le work hard.

[Exit.

SCÆNA SECUNDA

Enter **ANTIGONUS**, **MENIPPUS**, **2ND GENTLEMAN**, **LIEUTENANT** and **LORDS**.

ANTIGONUS
But is it possible this fellow took it?

2ND GENTLEMAN
It seems so by the violence it wrought with,
Yet now the fits ev'n off.

MENIPPUS
I beseech your Grace.

ANTIGONUS
Nay, I forgive thy wife with all my heart,
And am right glad she drank it not her self,
And more glad that the vertuous maid escap't it,
I would not for the world 'thad hit: but that this Souldier,
Lord how he looks, that he should take this vomit;
Can he make rimes too?

2ND GENTLEMAN
H'as made a thousand Sir,
And plaies the burthen to 'em on a Jews-trump,

ANTIGONUS

He looks as though he were bepist: do you love me Sir?

LIEUTENANT
Yes surely even with all my heart.

ANTIGONUS
I thank ye;
I am glad I have so good a subject: but pray ye tell me,
How much did ye love me, before ye drank this matter?

LIEUTENANT
Even as much as a sober man might; and a Souldier
That your grace owes just half a years pay to.

ANTIGONUS
Well remembred;
And did I seem so young and amiable to ye?

LIEUTENANT
Methought you were the sweetest youth—

ANTIGONUS
That's excellent.

LIEUTENANT
I truly Sir: and ever as I thought on ye,
I wished, and wished—

ANTIGONUS
What didst thou wish prethee?

LIEUTENANT
Ev'n, that I had been a wench of fifteen for ye,
A handsom wench Sir.

ANTIGONUS
Why? God a Mercy Souldier:
I seem not so now to thee.

LIEUTENANT
Not all out:
And yet I have a grudging to your grace still.

ANTIGONUS
Thou wast never in love before?

LIEUTENANT
Not with a King,

And hope I shall never be again: Truly Sir,
I have had such plunges, and such bickrings,
And as it were such runnings atilt within me,
For whatsoever it was provok't me toward ye.

ANTIGONUS
God a-mercy still.

LIEUTENANT
I had it with a vengeance,
It plaid his prize.

ANTIGONUS
I would not have been a wench then,
Though of this age.

LIEUTENANT
No sure, I should have spoil'd ye.

ANTIGONUS
Well, goe thy waies, of all the lusty lovers
That e're I saw—wilt have another potion?

LIEUTENANT
If you will be another thing, have at ye.

ANTIGONUS
Ha, ha, ha: give me thy hand, from henceforth thou art my souldier,
Do bravely, I'le love thee as much.

LIEUTENANT
I thank ye;
But if you were mine enemy, I would not wish it ye:
I beseech your Grace, pay me my charge.

2ND GENTLEMAN
That's certain Sir;
Ha's bought up all that e're he found was like ye,
Or any thing you have lov'd, that he could purchase;
Old horses, that your Grace has ridden blind, and foundr'd;
Dogs, rotten hawks, and which is more than all this,
Has worn your Grace's Gauntlet in his Bonnet.

ANTIGONUS
Bring in your Bills: mine own love shall be satisfi'd;
And sirrah, for this potion you have taken,
I'le point ye out a portion ye shall live on.

MENIPPUS
'Twas the best draught that e're ye drunk.

LIEUTENANT
I hope so.

ANTIGONUS
Are the Princes come to th' Court?

MENIPPUS
They are all, and lodg'd Sir.

ANTIGONUS
Come then, make ready for their entertainment,
Which presently we'l give: wait you on me Sir.

LIEUTENANT
I shall love drink the better whilst I live boyes.

[Exeunt.

SCÆNA TERTIA

Enter **DEMETRIUS** and **LEONTIUS**.

DEMETRIUS
Let me but see her, dear Leontius;
Let me but dye before her.

LEONTIUS
Would that would doe it:
If I knew where she lay now, with what honestie,
You having flung so main a mischief on her,
And on so innocent and sweet a Beauty,
Dare I present your visit?

DEMETRIUS
I'le repent all:
And with the greatest sacrifice of sorrow,
That ever Lover made.

LEONTIUS
'Twill be too late Sir:
I know not what will become of you.

DEMETRIUS

You can help me.

LEONTIUS
It may be to her sight: what are you nearer?
She has sworn she will not speak to ye, look upon ye,
And to love ye again, O she cries out, and thunders,
She had rather love—there is no hope—

DEMETRIUS
Yes Leontius,
There is a hope, which though it draw no love to it,
At least will draw her to lament my fortune,
And that hope shall relieve me.

LEONTIUS
Hark ye Sir, hark ye:
Say I should bring ye—

DEMETRIUS
Do not trifle with me?

LEONTIUS
I will not trifle; both together bring ye,
You know the wrongs ye' done.

DEMETRIUS
I do confess 'em.

LEONTIUS
And if you should then jump into your fury,
And have another querk in your head.

DEMETRIUS
I'le dye first.

LEONTIUS
You must say nothing to her; for 'tis certain,
The nature of your crime will admit no excuse.

DEMETRIUS
I will not speak, mine eyes shall tell my penance.

LEONTIUS
You must look wondrous sad too.

DEMETRIUS
I need not look so,
I am truly sadness self.

LEONTIUS
That look will do it:
Stay here, I'le bring her to you instantly:
But take heed how you bear your self: sit down there,
The more humble you are, the more she'l take compassion.
Women are per'lous things to deal upon.

[Exit.

DEMETRIUS
What shall become of me? to curse my fortune,
Were but to curse my Father; that's too impious;
But under whatsoever fate I suffer,
Bless I beseech thee heaven her harmless goodness.

[Enter **LEONTIUS** and **CELIA**.

LEONTIUS
Now arm your self.

CELIA
You have not brought him?

LEONTIUS
Yes faith,
And there he is: you see in what poor plight too,
Now you may doe your will, kill him, or save him.

CELIA
I will goe back.

LEONTIUS
I will be hang'd then Lady,
Are ye a coward now?

CELIA
I cannot speak to him.

DEMETRIUS
O me.

LEONTIUS
There was a sigh to blow a Church down;
So, now their eyes are fixt, the small shot playes,
They will come to th' batterie anon.

CELIA

He weeps extreamly.

LEONTIUS
Rail at him now.

CELIA
I dare not.

LEONTIUS
I am glad on't.

CELIA
Nor dare believe his tears.

DEMETRIUS
You may, blest beauty,
For those thick streams that troubled my repentance,
Are crept out long agoe.

LEONTIUS
You see how he looks.

CELIA
What have I to doe how he looks? how lookt he then,
When with a poisoned tooth he bit mine honour?
It was your counsel too, to scorn and slight him.

LEONTIUS
I, if ye saw fit cause; and you confest too,
Except this sin, he was the bravest Gentleman,
The sweetest, noblest: I take nothing from ye,
Nor from your anger; use him as you please:
For to say truth, he has deserved your justice;
But still consider what he has been to you.

CELIA
Pray do not blind me thus.

DEMETRIUS
O Gentle Mistris,
If there were any way to expiate
A sin so great as mine, by intercession,
By prayers, by daily tears, by dying for ye:
O what a joy would close these eyes that love ye.

LEONTIUS
They say women have tender hearts, I know not,
I am sure mine melts.

CELIA
Sir, I forgive ye heartily,
And all your wrong to me I cast behind me,
And wish ye a fit beauty to your vertues:
Mine is too poor, in peace I part thus from you;
I must look back: gods keep your grace: he's here still.

[Exit.

DEMETRIUS
She has forgiven me.

LEONTIUS
She has directed ye:
Up, up, and follow like a man: away Sir,
She lookt behind her twice: her heart dwells here Sir,
Ye drew tears from her too: she cannot freeze thus;
The door's set open too, are ye a man?
Are ye alive? do ye understand her meaning?
Have ye bloud and spirit in ye?

DEMETRIUS
I dare not trouble her.

LEONTIUS
Nay, and you will be nip't i'th' head with nothing,
Walk whining up and down; I dare not, I cannot:
Strike now or never: faint heart, you know what Sir—
Be govern'd by your fear, and quench your fire out.
A Devil on't, stands this door ope for nothing?
So get ye together, and be naught: now to secure all,
Will I go fetch out a more soveraign plaister.

[Exeunt.

SCÆNA QUARTA

Enter **ANTIGONUS, SELEUCUS, LYSIMACHUS, PTOLOMIE, LIEUTENANT, GENTLEMEN, LORDS**.

ANTIGONUS
This peace is fairly made.

SELEUCUS
Would your Grace wish us
To put in more: take what you please, we yield it;

The honour done us by your son constrains it,
Your noble son.

ANTIGONUS
It is sufficient, Princes;
And now we are one again, one mind, one body,
And one sword shall strike for us.

LYSIMACHUS
Let Prince Demetrius
But lead us on: for we are his vowed servants;
Against the strength of all the world we'l buckle.

PTOLOMIE
And even from all that strength we'l catch at victory.

SELECIUS
O had I now recover'd but the fortune
I lost in Antioch, when mine Unckle perish'd;
But that were but to surfeit me with blessings.

LYSIMACHUS
You lost a sweet child there.

SELECIUS
Name it no more Sir;
This is no time to entertain such sorrows;
Will your Majesty do us the honour, we may see the Prince,
And wait upon him?

[Enter **LEONTIUS**.

ANTIGONUS
I wonder he stayes from us:
How now Leontius, where's my son?

SELECIUS
Brave Captain.

LYSIMACHUS
Old valiant Sir.

LEONTIUS
Your Graces are welcom:
Your son and't please you Sir, is new cashiered yonder,
Cast from his Mistris favour: and such a coil there is;
Such fending, and such proving; she stands off,
And will by no means yield to composition:

He offers any price; his body to her.

SELECIUS
She is a hard Lady, denies that caution.

LEONTIUS
And now they whine, and now they rave: faith Princes,
'Twere a good point of charity to piece 'em;
For less than such a power will doe just nothing:
And if you mean to see him, there it must be,
For there will he grow, till he be transplanted.

SELECIUS
Beseech your grace, let's wait upon you thither,
That I may see that beauty dares deny him,
That scornfull beauty.

PTOLOMIE
I should think it worse now;
Ill brought up beauty.

ANTIGONUS
She has too much reason for't;
Which with too great a grief, I shame to think of,
But we'll go see this game.

LYSIMACHUS
Rather this wonder.

ANTIGONUS
Be you our guide Leontius, here's a new peace.

[Exit.

SCÆNA QUINTA

Enter **DEMETRIUS** and **CELIA**.

CELIA
Thus far you shall perswade me, still to honour ye,
Still to live with ye, Sir, or near about ye;
For not to lye, you have my first and last love:
But since you have conceiv'd an evil against me,
An evil that so much concerns your honour,
That honour aim'd by all at for a pattern:
And though there be a false thought, and confest too,

And much repentance faln in showrs to purge it;
Yet, whilest that great respect I ever bore ye,
Dwells in my bloud, and in my heart that duty;
Had it but been a dream, I must not touch ye.

DEMETRIUS
O you will make some other happy?

CELIA
Never,
Upon this hand I'le seal that faith.

DEMETRIUS
We may kiss,
Put not those out o'th' peace too.

CELIA
Those I'le give ye,
So there you will be pleas'd to pitch your ne ultra,
I will be merry with ye; sing, discourse with ye,
Be your poor Mistris still: in truth I love ye.

[Enter **LEONTIUS**, **ANTIGONUS**, **SELEUCUS**, **LYSIMACHUS**, **PTOLOMIE**, **LIEUTENANT** and **GENTLEMAN**.

DEMETRIUS
Stay, who are these?

LYSIMACHUS
A very handsom Lady.

LEONTIUS
As e're you saw.

SELECIUS
Pity her heart's so cruel.

LYSIMACHUS
How does your Grace? he stands still, will not hear us.

PTOLOMIE
We come to serve ye, Sir, in all our fortunes.

LYSIMACHUS
He bows a little now; he's strangely alter'd.

SELECIUS
Ha? pray ye a word Leontius, pray ye a word with ye,
Lysimachus? you bo'th knew mine Enanthe,

I lost in Antioch, when the Town was taken,
Mine Uncle slain, Antigonus had the sack on't?

LYSIMACHUS
Yes, I remember well the Girl.

SELECIUS
Methinks now
That face is wondrous like her: I have her picture,
The same, but more years on her; the very same.

LYSIMACHUS
A Cherry to a Chery is not liker.

SELECIUS
Look on her eyes.

LEONTIUS
Most certain she is like her:
Many a time have I dandled her in these arms, Sir,
And I hope who will more.

ANTIGONUS
What's that ye look at, Princes?

SELECIUS
This Picture, and that Lady, Sir.

ANTIGONUS
Ha! they are near:
They only err in time.

LYSIMACHUS
Did you mark that blush there?
That came the nearest.

SELECIUS
I must speak to her.

LEONTIUS
You'll quickly be resolved.

SELECIUS
Your name sweet Lady?

CELIA
Enanthe, Sir: and this to beg your blessing.

SELECIUS
Do you know me?

CELIA
If you be the King Seleucus,
I know you are my Father.

SELECIUS
Peace a little,
Where did I lose ye?

CELIA
At the Sack of Antioch,
Where my good Unckle di'd, and I was taken,
By a mean Souldier taken: by this Prince,
This noble Prince, redeem'd from him again,
Where ever since I have remain'd his Servant.

SELECIUS
My joys are now too full: welcome Enanthe,
Mine own, my dearest, and my best Enanthe.

DEMETRIUS
And mine too desperate.

SELECIUS
You shall not think so,
This is a peace indeed.

ANTIGONUS
I hope it shall be,
And ask it first.

CELIA
Most Royal Sir, ye have it.

DEMETRIUS
I once more beg it thus.

SELECIUS
You must not be deny'd, Sir.

CELIA
By me, I am sure he must not: sure he shall not;
Kneeling I give it too; kneeling I take it;
And from this hour, no envious spight e're part us.

ALL

The gods give happy joyes; all comforts to ye.

DEMETRIUS
My new Enanthe.

ANTIGONUS
Come, beat all the Drums up,
And all the noble instruments of War:
Let 'em fill all the Kingdom with their sound,
And those the brazen Arch of Heaven break through,
While to the Temple we conduct these two.

LEONTIUS
May they be ever loving, ever young,
And ever worthy of those lines they sprung;
May their fair issues walk with time along.

LIEUTENANT
And hang a Coward now; and there's my song.

[Exeunt.

EPILOGUE

Spoke by the **LIEUTENANT**.

I am not cur'd yet throughly; for believe
I feel another passion that may grieve,
All over me I feel it too: and now
It takes me cold, cold, cold, I know not how:
As you are good men help me, a Carowse
May make me love you all, all here i'th' house,
And all that come to see me doatingly;
Now lend your hands; and for your courtesie,
The next imployment I am sent upon,
I'le swear you are Physicians, the War's none.

John Fletcher – A Short Biography

John Fletcher was born in December, 1579 in Rye, Sussex. He was baptised on December 20th.

As can be imagined details of much of his life and career have not survived and, accordingly, only a very brief indication of his life and works can be given.

His father, Richard Fletcher, was a successful and rather ambitious cleric. From being the Dean of Peterborough he moved on to become the Bishop of Bristol, Bishop of Worcester and finally, shortly before his death, the Bishop of London. He was also the chaplain to Queen Elizabeth.

When he was Dean of Peterborough, Richard Fletcher, witnessed the execution of Mary, Queen of Scots. It was said he "knelt down on the scaffold steps and started to pray out loud and at length, in a prolonged and rhetorical style, as though determined to force his way into the pages of history". He cried out at her death, "So perish all the Queen's enemies!" All very dramatic but the family did have strong links to the Arts.

Young Fletcher appears at the very young age of eleven to have entered Corpus Christi College at Cambridge University in 1591. There are no records that he ever took a degree but there is some small evidence that he was being prepared for a career in the church.

However what is clear is that this was soon abandoned as he joined the stream of people who would leave University and decamp to the more bohemian life of commercial theatre in London.

Unfortunately his father fell out with Queen Elizabeth but appears to have been on his way to rehabilitation before his death in 1596. At his death he was, however, mired in debt.

The upbringing of the now teenage Fletcher and his seven siblings now passed to his paternal uncle, the poet and minor official Giles Fletcher. Giles, who had the patronage of the Earl of Essex may have been a liability rather than an advantage to the young Fletcher. With Essex involved in the failed rebellion against Elizabeth Giles was also tainted by association.

By 1606 John Fletcher appears to have equipped himself with the talents to become a playwright. Initially this appears to have been for the Children of the Queen's Revels, then performing at the Blackfriars Theatre.

Commendatory verses by Richard Brome in the Beaumont and Fletcher 1647 folio place Fletcher in the company of Ben Jonson, although it is not known when this friendship began. Jonson, of course, was a leviathan of English Literature, so admired that many of his literary friends and colleagues were simply known as 'Sons of Ben'. Fletcher's frequent early collaborator, Francis Beaumont, was also a friend of Jonson's.

Fletcher's early career was marked by one significant failure; The Faithful Shepherdess, his adaptation of Giovanni Battista Guarini's Il Pastor Fido, which was performed by the Blackfriars Children in 1608. In the preface to the printed edition of his play, Fletcher explained the failure as due to his audience's faulty expectations. They expected a pastoral tragicomedy to feature dances, comedy, and murder, with the shepherds presented in conventional stereotypes – as Fletcher put it, wearing "gray cloaks, with curtailed dogs in strings." Fletcher's preface is however best known for its pithy definition of tragicomedy: "A tragicomedy is not so called in respect of mirth and killing, but in respect it wants [i.e., lacks] deaths, which is enough to make it no tragedy; yet brings some near it, which is enough to make it no comedy." A comedy, he went on to say, must be "a representation of familiar people." His preface is critical of drama that features characters whose action violates nature.

In that case, Fletcher appears to have been developing a new style faster than audiences could comprehend. By 1609, however, he had found his stride. With Beaumont, he wrote Philaster, which became a hit for the King's Men and began a profitable association between Fletcher and that company. Philaster appears also to have begun a trend for tragicomedy. Fletcher's influence has also been said to have inspired some features of Shakespeare's late romances, and certainly his influence on the tragicomic work of other playwrights is even more marked.

By the middle of the 1610s, Fletcher's plays had achieved a popularity that rivalled Shakespeare's and cemented the pre-eminence of the King's Men in Jacobean London. After Beaumont's retirement, necessitated by ill-health, and then his early death in 1616, Fletcher continued working, both singly and in collaboration, until his death in 1625. By that time, he had produced, or had been credited with, close to fifty plays. This body of work remained a major part of the King's Men's repertory until the closing of the theatres in 1642 due to the Civil War.

At the beginning of his career Fletcher's most important collaborator was Francis Beaumont. The two wrote together for close to a decade, first for the Children of the Queen's Revels, and then for the King's Men. According to an anecdote transmitted or invented by John Aubrey, they also lived together in Bankside, sharing clothes and having "one wench in the house between them." This domestic arrangement, if it existed, was ended by Beaumont's marriage in 1613, and their dramatic partnership ended after Beaumont fell ill, probably of a stroke, that same year.

At this point Fletcher had written many plays with Beaumont and several others on his own. He seems to have been regarded as quite a talent although it should be remembered that playwrights were required to be prolific, to easily work with other collaborators and to produce work of quality and commercial appeal very quickly.

The King's Men, run by Philip Henslowe, was the most prestigious of the theatre companies and Fletcher now had an increasingly close association with it.

Fletcher collaborated with Shakespeare on Henry VIII, The Two Noble Kinsmen, and the now lost Cardenio, which some scholars say was the basis for Lewis Theobald's play Double Falsehood. (Theobald is regarded as one of the best Shakespearean editors. Whether his play is based on Cardenio or on some other is not absolutely known although Theobald certainly promoted it as his revision of the lost Shakespeare/Fletcher play.)

A play that Fletcher also wrote by himself at this time, The Woman's Prize or the Tamer Tamed, is also regarded as a sequel to The Taming of the Shrew.

In 1616, with the death of Shakespeare, Fletcher now appears to have entered into an enhanced arrangement with the King's Men on very similar terms to Shakespeare's. Fletcher would now write exclusively for the King's Men until his own death almost a decade later.

As well as continuing his solo productions Fletcher was still collaborating with other playwrights, mainly Philip Massinger, who, in turn, would succeed him as the in-house playwright for the King's Men.

Fletcher's popularity continued throughout his life; indeed during the winter of 1621, he had three of his plays performed at court. His mastery is most notable in two dramatic types; tragicomedy and the comedy of manners.

John Fletcher died in 1625, it is thought of bubonic plague which, at the time, was undergoing further outbreaks.

He seems to have been buried in what is now Southwark Cathedral, although a precise location is not known. There is much made of an anecdote that Fletcher and Massinger (who died in 1640) share the same grave but it is more likely that both are buried within a few yards of each other and that the stone markers in the floor have confused the issue. One is marked 'Edmond Shakespeare 1607' and the other 'John Fletcher 1625' refers to Shakespeare's younger brother and the playwright. The churchyards were, more often than not, completely over-crowded and breeding grounds for disease. Precise record keeping was not a practiced skill.

During the later Commonwealth, many of the playwright's best-known scenes were kept alive as drolls. These were brief performances, usually condensed into one or two scenes and with the addition of music or song to satisfy the taste for plays while the theatres were closed under the Puritans. At the re-opening of the theatres in 1660, the plays in the Fletcher canon, in original form or revised, were by far the most common productions on the English stage. The most frequently revived plays suggest the developing taste for comedies of manners. Among the tragedies, The Maid's Tragedy and, especially, Rollo Duke of Normandy held the stage. Four tragicomedies (A King and No King, The Humorous Lieutenant, Philaster, and The Island Princess) were popular, perhaps in part for their similarity to and foreshadowing of heroic drama. Four comedies (Rule a Wife And Have a Wife, The Chances, Beggars' Bush, and especially The Scornful Lady) were also stage mainstays.

Despite his popularity, and it appears he was held in higher regard than Shakespeare at this time, his works steadily lost ground to those of Shakespeare and to new productions from other playwrights.

Since then Fletcher has increasingly become a subject only for occasional revivals and for specialists. Fletcher and his collaborators have been the subject of important bibliographic and critical studies, but the plays have been revived only infrequently.

Due to the frequent collaborations between all manner of playwrights, and the revisions carried out in later years, having a settled list of authorship to any given set of plays can be problematic. The works of Fletcher and others of this period most definitely fall into this category. It is as well to take into account that during this period theatres were quite often closed either due to outbreaks of the plague or to the prevailing political and moral climate. Printers, anxious to provide materials that would sell, were not above changing a name or two to enhance sales.

Although Fletcher collaborated most often with Beaumont and Massinger, it is believed that Massinger revised many of the plays some time after their original production. Other collaborators including Nathan Field, William Shakespeare, William Rowley and others also can be seen distinctly in Fletchers' works. Many modern scholars point out that Fletcher had many particular mannerisms but other playwrights would also duplicate these at times so allocating exact contributions of anyone to a play is somewhat of a detective case in many instances. However from the original folio printings or licensing via the Master of the Revels (the statutory licensing authority to approve and censor plays as well a hand in publication and printing of theatrical materials) as well as contemporary notes a fairly precise bibliography of the works can be given with only a few plays lacking substantial authority and provenance.

John Fletcher – A Concise Bibliography

This bibliography gives the most likely date of writing together with when published, revised or licensed by the Master or the Revels (This position within the royal household was originally for royal festivities, ie revels, and later to oversee stage censorship, until this function was transferred to the Lord Chamberlain in 1624).

Solo Plays

The Faithful Shepherdess, pastoral (written 1608–9; printed 1609)
The Tragedy of Valentinian, tragedy (1610–14; 1647)
Monsieur Thomas, comedy (c. 1610–16; 1639)
The Woman's Prize, or The Tamer Tamed, comedy (c. 1611; 1647)
Bonduca, tragedy (1611–14; 1647)
The Chances, comedy (c. 1613–25; 1647)
Wit Without Money, comedy (c. 1614; 1639)
The Mad Lover, tragicomedy (acted 5 January 1617; 1647)
The Loyal Subject, tragicomedy (licensed 16 November 1618; revised 1633; 1647)
The Humorous Lieutenant, tragicomedy (c. 1619; 1647)
Women Pleased, tragicomedy (c. 1619–23; 1647)
The Island Princess, tragicomedy (c. 1620; 1647)
The Wild Goose Chase, comedy (c. 1621; 1652)
The Pilgrim, comedy (c. 1621; 1647)
A Wife for a Month, tragicomedy (licensed 27 May 1624; 1647)
Rule a Wife and Have a Wife, comedy (licensed 19 October 1624; 1640)

Collaborations

With Francis Beaumont

The Woman Hater, comedy (1606; 1607)
Cupid's Revenge, tragedy (c. 1607–12; 1615)
Philaster, or Love Lies a-Bleeding, tragicomedy (c. 1609; 1620)
The Maid's Tragedy, Tragedy (c. 1609; 1619)
A King and No King, tragicomedy (1611; 1619)
The Captain, comedy (c. 1609–12; 1647)
The Scornful Lady, comedy (c. 1613; 1616)
Love's Pilgrimage, tragicomedy (c. 1615–16; 1647)
The Noble Gentleman, comedy (c. 1613; licensed 3 February 1626; 1647)

With Francis Beaumont & Philip Massinger

Thierry & Theodoret, tragedy (c. 1607; 1621)
The Coxcomb, comedy (c. 1608–10; 1647)
Beggars' Bush, comedy (c. 1612–13; revised 1622; 1647)
Love's Cure, comedy (c. 1612–13; revised 1625; 1647)

With Philip Massinger

Sir John van Olden Barnavelt, tragedy (August 1619; MS)

The Little French Lawyer, comedy (c. 1619–23; 1647)
A Very Woman, tragicomedy (c. 1619–22; licensed 6 June 1634; 1655)
The Custom of the Country, comedy (c. 1619–23; 1647)
The Double Marriage, tragedy (c. 1619–23; 1647)
The False One, history (c. 1619–23; 1647)
The Prophetess, tragicomedy (licensed 14 May 1622; 1647)
The Sea Voyage, comedy (licensed 22 June 1622; 1647)
The Spanish Curate, comedy (licensed 24 October 1622; 1647)
The Lovers' Progress or The Wandering Lovers, tragicomedy (licensed 6 December 1623; rev 1634; 1647)
The Elder Brother, comedy (c. 1625; 1637)

With Philip Massinger & Nathan Field
The Honest Man's Fortune, tragicomedy (1613; 1647)
The Queen of Corinth, tragicomedy (c. 1616–18; 1647)
The Knight of Malta, tragicomedy (c. 1619; 1647)

With William Shakespeare
Henry VIII, history (c. 1613; 1623)
The Two Noble Kinsmen, tragicomedy (c. 1613; 1634)
Cardenio, tragicomedy (c. 1613)

With Thomas Middleton & William Rowley
Wit at Several Weapons, comedy (c. 1610–20; 1647)

With William Rowley
The Maid in the Mill (licensed 29 August 1623; 1647).

With Nathan Field
Four Plays, or Moral Representations, in One, morality (c. 1608–13; 1647)

With Philip Massinger, Ben Jonson and George Chapman
Rollo Duke of Normandy, or The Bloody Brother, tragedy (c. 1617; revised 1627–30; 1639)

With James Shirley
The Night Walker, or The Little Thief, comedy (c. 1611; 1640)
The Coronation c. 1635

Uncertain
The Nice Valour, or The Passionate Madman, comedy (c. 1615–25; 1647)
The Laws of Candy, tragicomedy (c. 1619–23; 1647)
The Fair Maid of the Inn, comedy (licensed 22 January 1626; 1647)
The Faithful Friends, tragicomedy (registered 29 June 1660; MS.)

The Nice Valour is possibly by Fletcher revised by Thomas Middleton;

The Fair Maid of the Inn is perhaps a play by Massinger, John Ford, and John Webster, either with or without Fletcher's involvement.

The Laws of Candy has been variously attributed to Fletcher and to John Ford.

The Night-Walker was a Fletcher original, with additions by Shirley for a 1639 production.

Even now there is not absolute certainty on several of the plays. The first Beaumont & Fletcher folio of 1647 contained 35 plays and the second folio of 1679 added a further 18. In total 53 plays.

The first folio included The Masque of the Inner Temple and Gray's Inn (1613), and the second The Knight of the Burning Pestle (1607), widely considered Beaumont's solo works, although the latter was in early editions attributed to both writers. Fletcher himself said that Beaumont was attributed so-authorship of many works that belonged solely to Fletcher or to other collaborators.

One play in the canon, Sir John Van Olden Barnavelt, existed in manuscript and was not published till 1883.

www.ingramcontent.com/pod-product-compliance
Lightning Source LLC
Chambersburg PA
CBHW061441040426
42450CB00007B/1161